# A GLOSSARY OF SLANG PERSIAN WORDS

## in phonetic alphabet

With Etymologic and Semantic Remarks

by
### Jami Gilani Shakibi, MD
With collaboration of
### Bahram Youssefi, AIA

2nd Revision
Nashville, U.S.A. and Shemiran, Iran 1988
1st edition 2011, Maryland U.S.A.

Publisher: Babylonia Language and Translation Center, Inc.
Title: A Glossary of Slang Persian Words
Copyright © 2011 Jami Gilani Shakibi, MD
Author: Jami Gilani Shakibi MD
First edition 2011
Printed by: Createspace
Library of Congress Registration number TXu 1-760-451
ISBN 978-0-9841498-3-4

# PREFACE

While compiling and editing "a Concise Etymologic Dictionary of The Persian Language", and "Zarbiz e Pársi", I realized that some ultra-slang terms, usually omitted from the dictionaries, or treated very perfunctorily, have very deep and solid etymologic roots. A few examples will put this point in the highlight:

"Besse!" in "Uno besse!" "Look at him"! is made of "be-" a verbal particle, and "se", derived from "sahidan" or "sahestan", a Pahlavi word, meaning "to seem, to seem proper". (MK. P 73)

"Xow o bew kardim", "bew" is the same word as Pahlavi "bew" and "viw" (MK p.18; BF p.96) meaning" sorrow", "pain" etc.

"Váse ye man" "for me", "bosaw" "for him". "Váse" or "bose" is derived from "vasnád" again a Pahlavi word meaning "for...", "on account of..." (MK p.88, BF p.583)

Compilation of the Persian slang words and terms is an immense task, and is beyond the scope of the present work. My goal in this treatise is only limited to a number of ultra-slang words. Before attempting to find and track the origins and roots of these words, a clear definition of these items is necessary. As most translations of these words in other languages are inaccurate, I try, to the best of my ability, to find examples of the use of these terms and elucidate their meanings in practical settings. In many instances I have explained the circumstances where these words or terms are used, rather than giving an "equivalent" English term, which is in most instances partially true, and thus usually misleading. Except in a few instances words of onomatopoeic origin are omitted.

Except where noted, all etymologic derivations and semantic reconstructions are my original work and proposals, presented as hypotheses for future research, to be confirmed or rejected.

A phonetic alphabet is used for correct pronunciation of the Persian words. This alphabet was originally proposed by A. Kasravi, and subsequently completed by the author.

The following phonetic alphabet proposed by A. Kasravi, is used for correct pronunciation of the Persian words.

برای درست خواندن واژه ها از دبیره ی آوایی (phonetic alphabet) زیر پیشنهادی کسروی کمک گرفته شده است.

| proposed alphabet | sounds like | in the word | in Persian |
|---|---|---|---|
| **A - a** | **a** | and | مانند "اِ" در "اسب" |
| **Á - á** | **a** | are | مانند "آ" در "آب" |
| **B - b** | **b** | bed | مانند "ب" در "بز" |
| **C - c** | **ch** | cheese | مانند "چ" در "چشم" |
| **D - d** | **d** | door | مانند "د" در "دست" |
| **E - e** | **e** | end | مانند "اِ" در "امروز" |
| **F - f** | **f** | far | مانند "ف" در "فرزند" |
| **G - g** | **g** | go | مانند "گ" در "گل" |
| **H - h** | **h** | head | مانند "ه" در "هیزم" |
| **I - i** | **ee** | see | مانند "ی" در "تیغ" |
| **J - j** | **j** | jar | مانند "ج" در "جنگ" |
| **K - k** | **k** | kill | مانند "ک" در "کلم" |
| **L - l** | **l** | lip | مانند "ل" در "لب" |
| **M - m** | **m** | man | مانند "م" در "من" |
| **N - n** | **n** | name | مانند "ن" در "نام" |
| **O - o** | **o** | door | مانند "اُ" در "اردک" |
| **P - p** | **p** | pie | مانند "پ" در "پدر" |
| **Q - q** | **r** (in French) | rose | مانند "غ" در "غبار" |
| **R - r** | **r** (in Spanish) | burro | مانند "ر" در "روز" |
| **S - s** | **s** | sit | مانند "س" در "سیم" |
| **T - t** | **t** | tea | مانند "ت" در "تب" |
| **U - u** | **oo** | root | مانند "و" در "توت" |
| **V - v** | **v** | very | مانند "و" در "آوند" |
| **W - w** | **sh** | shoe | مانند "ش" در "شب" |
| **X - x** | **ch** (in German) | Buch | مانند "خ" در "خواب" |
| **Y - y** | **y** | yellow | مانند "ی" در "یک" |
| **Z - z** | **z** | zebra | مانند "ز" در "زور" |
| **Ź - ź** | **j** (in French) | jolie | مانند "ژ" در "آژند" |

Additional characters added to the phonetic alphabet:

Read "**d́**" as "th" in the English word "that".

Read "**t́**" as "th" in the English word "thin".

Read "**v́**" as "w" in English word "win"

Note the formation of the following diphthongs by the vowels:

Read "**ay**" as "ei" in German "Eimer"    Read "**ya**" as "ya" in "yank"

Read "**áy**" as "ie" in "lie"    Read "**yá**" as "ya" in "yard"

Read "**ey**" as "ai" in "rain"    Read "**ye**" as "ye" in "yes"

Read "**iy**" not used as diphthong    Read "**yi**" as "yea" in "yeast"

Read "**oy**" as "oy" in "boy"    Read "**yo**" as "yo" in "York"

Read "**uy**" as "uee" in "queen"    Read "**yu**" as "yu" in "yule"

Read "**ou**" as "ow" in "row"

In the above diphthongs, "i" could replace "y".

1- We introduce a "y" between "i" and a following vowel, such as: miya'n(ميان) ; siyah(سیه); viyolon(ویلون).

2- We use apostrophe(') to represent eyn(ع), hamze(ء) or glottal stop wherever it is needed: mo-,áhede (معاهده); a-,zá (اعضاء); bá-,es (باعث); mas-,ul (مسؤل); ro-,us (رئوس); bel-,axare (بالاخره).

3- "yi" is used to represent the suffix made of "ye and ye" "یی" or "alef(الف) and ye" "ای" such as: boxári(بخاری) and boxáriyi gázi (بخاریی گازی); xáne(خانه) and xáneyi zibá (خانه ای زیبا)

4- Genitive case, particle "e" is written separately: deraxt e sabz (درخت سبز). If the substantive ends in a vowel, a "y" is added to "e" such as: nuwábe <u>ye</u> sard (نوشابه ی سرد)

5- Attached separate words shall be written with a hyphen between them: az án(از آن) or z-án (زان); ze in(ز این) or z-in(زین), ke in(که این) or k-in (کاین); man ham(من هم) or man-am(منم) (colloquial)

6- Hyphen is used in colloquial Persian, in writing verbs such as: Deraxt-e. (درخت است.), Máhi-ye. (ماهی است.), Man-am. (من هستم.)

7- The suffixes of definite article (-e or -he) are attached to their substantives: Máwine rá didi (آن گربه را گرفتی); Gorbehe rá gerefti (آن ماشین را دیدی)

8- The suffixes of indefinite article (-i or -yi) are attached to their substantives: ketábi; turiyi catri; xáneyi

The following signs are used in this text:

< = derived from

≡ = equivalent of

√ = a radical or root

* = a hypothetical word or base

[…] = author's view or hypothesis.

cf or § = compare

The following abbreviations are used for the following references:

B : borhán e Qáte, edited by: Dr. Mohammad Moin. Fifth edition 1362, Amir Kabir Publishing House, Tehran.

FM : Fanhang e Moin: by Dr. Mohammad Moin. Fourth edition. 1360, Amir Kabir Publishing House, Tehran.

BF : Farhang e Zabán e Pahlavi, by Dr. Bahram Faravashi. Third Edition, Tehran University press, 1358.

MK : A Concise Pahlavi dictionary: by D.N. MacKenzie, Oxford University Press, London 1971.

# A

## ADÁ

"xow-adá": *One who has pleasant and sweet gestures.*
Ádam e bad-adáyi-ye": *One who finds faults with everything and is hard to please.*
"Adá ye mádarew o darmiyare. *"He imitates his mother."*
"Jelo ye áyne newaste adá darmiyáre". *"She is sitting in front of the mirror and makes faces."*
"adá" ? < (adá) *(Arabic) (to perform)*

## ALAKI

"Alaki goft." *His statement was groundless.*
"Alaki-ye." *It is phony.*
"Pas alalki umadim?" *So we came for no good reason?*
*etymology*:
[cf "halak" *(Pahlavi): mad, crazy, stupid, irresponsible (BF p.241). cf harza; harze; wer; kos-wer*
*See "hale-hule", for further etymologic discussion.*]

## ALEMOZQE

*This term is used when referring to or making a remark about somebody who is apparently of low caliber, or mediocre capability and who interferes with some work requiting higher qualities. Thus "Mardeke ye alemozqe az doxtar e man xástegári karde…" "The unworthy man has asked for the hand of my daughter."*
[*etymology*: alemozqe *cf ali varje, ale, are, harz, alaki: useless, worthless,idle*
"mozqe" *omit "e" suffix,* "mozq" *cf* "maxk", *"mask"*
"mawk" – *a leather water bottle, a leather sack for churning milk*
maske 1- *Butter obtained from milk by churning it.* 2- "maske zadan" *to shake a leather sack, in order to obtain butter from milk.*
*thus*: "ale-mozq-e": *One who idly churns a leather sack, thus worthless person. One who has no decent job.*]

1

## ALOU = ÁLÁV

"Naft alou gereft." *"The kerosene caught fire and burned in a blaze."*
"Alou alou, ba-, ze (beh az, behtar az) polou!" *(In cold weather this expression is used to praise the fire.) "flame of fire, flame of fire, (is) better than cooked rice!"*
"alou zadan": "alou zad be tanew." *"The flame of fire touched his body."*
[*etymology: < ? cf* ál; *cf* हरि *hari (Sanskrit)(fire)*]

## AN

*This word refers to semisolid feces. Feces or excrement not watery but not hard either. Feces of creamy consistency. Figuratively anything disgusting. Also "an damáq", "mucous discharge from the nose."*
"Rixtew be an mimune!" *"His facies is like semisolid stool." Thus, "He is very ugly and unseemly and moody."*
*etymology:? Cf* havu.

## ANCUCAK

*This word is used as a substantive. It is pejorative and refers to somebody usually of young age and small stature who interferes with works not directly of his business or concern, or too big for his caliber or size.*
"Martike ye ancucak be kár e man fozuli mikone!" *"The unworthy, despicable midget puts his nose into my business!"*
[*etymology: Although* "ancucak" *means* "pear seed", *I believe that his meaning has nothing to do with* "ancucak" *as an ultra-slang term.*
?an-cuc-ak: "an" *see* "an" *"semisolid stool";* cuc-ak, *cf* juj-a *(chicken) or cf* cuźa, cuz-a *(chicken) or* źuź-a, *(porcupine), Chicken or porcupine's droppings.*]

## ANG

"Bará ye yeqqerun ang mindáze." *This term is used to show extreme poverty and need.* "ang endáxtan", *to use a hook for fishing out something, as if from a well etc. "He is so needy that he will try to fish out a cent (from a well)."*
[*etymology and semantic reconstruction: From the meanings given in FM, p.388, ie: 1-honey bee, 2-Juice, extract, 3-clay water-pipe, 4-trademark, to put trademark on products, none lends itself to* "ang" *as used in Persian slang.*
"ang" *in Isfahani dialect means,* "grapevine sprout", *"A sprout of grapevine before bearing grapes".* ang[1] = *juice, sap.* ang[2] = ang *in Isfahani dialect. This*

*is the basis for semantic reconstruction of* "ang", *(BF, p27)* ["ang": *primary concept: Any finger-like projection, sharp, pointed or goad-like object.*]

[ang-owt: अंगुलि ánguli: अंगुष्ट anguwta *(Sanskrit) (finger)*

ang-ul-ak: अंगुशः ánguwah *(a hook, a goad); to poke with finger, to tinker with something; to manipulate.)*

ang-ul: अंकुरीः ángurih; *(see angulak) (sprout, shoot, blade, in compound words, pointed, sharp)*

ang-ván: *asa faetida (Latin).* and-, ang[1]- *juice* + źad

ang[1] ang-źad+van = van = *tree*-zád: źad *(resin);* and-,

ang[1]+-al: *a parasite. Anything hanging to others as if with hook-like or finger-like projections.*

Thus "ang andáxtan": *to use a hook or goad-like object for fishing out objects.*]

## ANGULAK

"Carx o angulak nakoni" *"don't tinker with the machine!" "Don't poke your finger into the machine!"*

"Neweste o bacca ro angulak mikone!" *"He is constantly busy messing with (or fingering) the child."*

*etymology: See* "ang".

## ARNAUD

*(of men and women: rogue; vicious malicious; wicked)*
*This is a pejorative term.*
*example:* "Ye barádar e arnaudi dáre.)*(She/He has a wicked brother)*
[*etymology ?: √?*]

## ATAL

"Atal metal tutule"
*Meaning and semantic reconstruction: in contrast to the commonly held view that the children's songs and expressions are meaningless (given in the example below), the author believes that these expressions are based on solid linguistic grounds.* "Qáleb e aw^ár e atal-matal-mánand ma^ni ye manteqi va rouwani nadárand, vazn va bázihá ye souti ast ke ánhá rá matlub e baccehá mikonad...." (Ehsán e Yárwáter, Iran-Náme, No. 3, 1367, p369)
[*etymology*: atal...= ázar *(fire)*
matal: *novel, story*
tut = dud *(smoke)*

3

ule = áre (*brings*) - *or cf* kutule, kuculu-muculu (*small smoke*)
*or*: tutul, *cf* dudul, -ul, -ule, *suffix of smallness*: tutule: *small smoke or causes
smoke, brings smoke.*]
*This expression is used in children's play, with everybody sitting on the floor
with extended legs. Somebody while singing this song and its continuation,
eliminates the legs of the children one by one, all the way down to the last one.
The owner of the very last leg is tickled. The legs of children being quite
similar to logs and firewood adds additional support to the etymologic and
semantic hypothesis proposed above. (JGS)*

## ATFÁR = ATVÁR

"Atfár" *is used to signify coquettish gestures. Figuratively it means: "to be
malfunctioning." "*Doxtara ro bebin ce atvár miyád." *Look at the chick who
has a coquettish manner." "*Báz in máwin atfár miyád.", *"This machine or car
is malfunctioning repeatedly." "*Báz in máwin atvár mirize." *"Again this car
or machine is malfunctioning and stopping off and on." "*atvár ámadan" =
"atvár rixtan" *1- to behave coquettishly, 2- to malfunction repeatedly.*
[*etymology:*? < atvár (*Arabic*) < *tour: 1- way, 2 – manner, 3 – behavior*]

## ATVÁR

*See* "atfár".

## AXM

*Frown, frowning.* "Axm nakon!" *Don't frown!" "Don't make a sad face!"*
"axm kardan" *"to make a sad or solemn face." "*axm o taxm": *frowning and/
or showing a solemn or sad face. This may be associated with occasional
insulting remarks or gestures.* "axm o taxm kardan" *"to behave or to treat
someone angrily." "*Bá axm o taxm goft." *"He said angrily".* "axmu"
*somebody who is morose and of depressed or solemn mood most of the times.*
[*etymology:* "axm: ax-m; ax < axv, axv́" < ?, "tahm" *cf* "dam", "dame",
"damaq". *All related with* तमस् támás (*Sanskrit*) *dark, (nature). See* "damaq".]

# Á

**ÁBJI** = báji *(sister-)*
"Bá ábjiw raft bázár." *"He went to bazaar with his/her sister."*
*etymology:* ábji = ábáji = báji. भगिनी bhágini, भग्नी bhágni *(Sanskrit) sister.*
ábáji *(Turkish) < see above.*]

## ÁB-LAMBU

*see* "lombar"
*The most typical example is:* "anár e áb-lambu" *i.e. a pommegranate which is squeezed gently, so the juice is collected inside its unbroken skin.* "Áb-lambu", *is thus anything which could fluctuate under an examining finger. In medicine* "caput succedaneum" *(a bleeding under the scalp of a newborn) is* "áb-lambu". *A rotten melon may also be referred to as* "áb-lambu wode."
[*etymology and semantic reconstruction: Also see* "lombar"
áb, = *water, juice, exudate*
lambu, -u *(suffix) This suffix confers a quality in its extreme to something, thus:*
"riwu" *(having a luxurious beard);* riqu *(puny, one who has emaciated due to chronic diarrhea):* "guzu *(one who emits lots of gas, one who farts, big farter):*
lamb-, ≡ *dom, domb, donb:* duma-, *(Avest)(tall) (BQM p.876)*
[*etymologic and Semantic reconstruction:*
lomb-ar: *a fat buttock or ass.*
do-lonb-e: *fat, rotund, plump*
domb: *a tail*
dombe, donbe: *the fatty tail of asian sheep.*
qo-lonb-e: *a round protruding mass*
cf. damávand, = donb-ávand *cf* nehá-vand. (Kárvand e Kasravi).
donb-al, domal *(an abscess)*
donb-al-án: *(1- testes of sheep or oxen. 2- large round mushroom)*
donb-ál-ce = donb-ol-ice *(an appendix, a small round appendix)*]

## ÁB-O-TÁB

"bá áb-o-táb goftan": *to describe in a detailed and grandiloquent manner.* "áb-o-táb dádan" *To tell in a detailed manner, expecially to attract the attention.*

[*etymology*: áb (brilliance, luster): ábhá *(Sanskrit)(brilliance)*.  táb < ताप: tápáh *(heat) (Sanskrit)*
*semantic reconstruction*: áb-o-táb; tábidan; táftan; tábe; tab; taft; taftidan; áftáb; taf-sidan]

## ÁKELE

"zanike ye ákele": *This is a typical example.  The word is generally used to describe a woman who is rude, not very young or beautiful, who is obsessed with sex.*
*etymology*: "ákele" < ákele *(Arabic) (eater)(feminine)* < "akl" *(to eat).  In Persian* "ákele" *is also used for* "leprosy", *a mutilating disease of the limbs.*

## ÁL

1- Ál-o-palangi, *or* ále-palangi, "Cerá piráhan e ále-palangi puwidi?"  *"Why did you put on a very colorful shirt?"*  "Ále-palangi" *is used to refer to all material with coarse, and large designs in very bright and flashy colors, especially red or pink.*
2- Ál-zade: "Pas az záyemun ál zadew."  *"After child-birth, she became ill and had seizures."*  ("Ál" *in this case is synonymous with* "genie" *a minor devil or a subordinate of Satan."*  "Rixtew mese ál mimune."  *"She has a demonical facies.  She is ugly and unkempt."*
[*etymology*: "Ál" *in its major and primary concept is a minor devil.  The devil is typically red.  The T.V. serial of* "Pink Panther" *is striking.  The title closely corresponds with* "ále-palangi". *Did the author of the T.V. serial cartoon, get an inspiration from* "ál"?! "ále-palangi" *or* "ál-o-palangi" *"mottled red".*
*Cf* ál *with* अरुस् árus *(Sanskrit): red.*
*Cf* ál *with* "áláv" = alou *(the flame of a fire; a blaze)*]

## ÁLÁV

*See* "alou".

## ÁPÁRTI

*(shrew; lewd ; immoral)*
*This is a pejorative term. It is commonly applied to girls or women who are of indecent manners ,usually promiscuous, foul-mouthed and of indecent manners.*
*example*: "In zanike ye ápárti pedar e man o darávorde." *(This shrew has given*

*me very hard time.)*
*etymology:* √?

## ÁS-O-PÁS

*Cf* lát-o-pát. "ás-o-pás" *means, somebody without any money.* "Hey qomár kard tá ás-o-pás wod." *"He gambled a lot and became a destitute."*
[*etymology:* √?
"ás": *cf* "ásemán", "ás", "áhan" *all* < "asman" *(Avest.)*; अश्मन *"áwmán"* *(Sanskrit)(stone).*]

## ÁZEGÁR; ÁZGÁR

*This is an adjective always following another term describing a period of time, such as:* "dah hafte" *(ten weeks),* "panj sál" *(five years) etc. the combination of any expression of time with* "ázegár", *with the help of* "e" *the sign of genitive case or attribute, gives the impression of the entire length of time (usually considered too long), associated with continuous suffering.*
"dah sál e ázegár jang bud." *"For ten uninterrupted years, there was war."* or *"there was continuous war for ten years."* "Dah ruz e ázegár tewne mundim." *"We were thirsty and without access to water for ten long days." Or "there was no access to water for ten days."*
[*etymology:* √? *cf* ámuz(e)gár; (kerde)gár; ruzegár; áfaridegár
-gár = gar: rixtegar; bázigar; pilegar
*-doer, maker*
áz-,; *cf* ád-,; ás-,: *to eat: consume*
ázgár, ázegar: *consuming; exhausting*]

# B

## BALVÁ

"Nemiduni ce baváyi wod!" *"You can't imagine, what a riot (there was)!"*
"balvá wod." *"There was a riot." "There was a noisy confusion."*
"Dar balvá ye Xorásán sad tan kowte wodand." *"100 people were killed in the riots of Khorasan."*
*etymology: "balvá is derived from arabic "balvá"*

## BANDIL

*Also see "bár o bandil".*
"Bár o bandilew o bast raft." *"He packed up all his loads and possessions and left."*
"bandil" *is almost always used in the form of "bár o bandil" where "bár" means "load" and "bandil" means "case, chest, possessions"*
[*etymology*: "bandil" = band-il
"band" < √ बंध् *bándh, (to bind, tie, fasten)*
भांड *bhanda (Sanskrit):* -a vessel, pot (cf "ávand")
            -a box, trunk, chest, case
            -goods, wares, merchandise, shopkeeper's stock.
            - a bale of goods
            -any valued possession, treasures]

## BA-, ZE

*See "áláv" = "alou". "ba-, ze" = beh az = beh ze (better than)*
"Har ce xub báwe ba-, ze to ke nemiwe." *"Even though she is good, however she cannot be your match; she cannot be better than you."*
"Sagew ba-, ze xodew-e!" *"His dog is better than he, himself!" (He is of bad mood and temper.)*

## BÁBÁQURI

*This work is used as a substantive meaning "blind in one eye".*
"zad tu cewew, bábáquri wod!" *"He was hit in the eye, and he became blind in one eye."*
"Bábáquri ro besse!" *"Watch the one-eyed-man!"*

8

"Xodá az cewm e bábáquri hefzet kone!" *"May god protect you from the evil effect of the blind eye!" (This is said about somebody who is mean, greedy and malicious. The expression is a sarcastic remark.)*
*[etymology: bábá = man, father*
*"Quri" is directly derived from "kur" (blind) and "kuri" (blindness).]*

## BÁJI

*(A sister, nurse-maid, woman) see: ábáji, ábji. (This is a depreciative term for "womá" or "lady")*
"In bimárestán bejá ye parastár báji dáre." *(This hospital has no trained nurses.)*
"Az dard e bi aláji be gorbe goftam xám-báji!" *(Being extremely lonely, I called the cat, "landlady"!)(anybody, even a cat, could be my companion.)*
*etymology: See "ábji, ábáji".*

## BÁK

Bákew nist!" *(He is not touched or moved by a serious incident.) (He does not give a damn!) (He is not at all scared, He doesn't think about it.)*
*Also used with the privative particle, "bi-," "bibák". "Bibák" = bold, rash, not thinking about consequences of one's actins, fearless.*
*[etymology: cf* भी *bhi = to fear;* भी: *bhih = fear;* भयं *bháyán (Sanskrit) = fear.*
*Also cf "bim", "bime", also: "báyaka" (Old Persian)]*

## BÁMBUL

*Used in the forms of* "bámbul zadan" *and* "bámbul darávardan".
"Har ce gofam ye bámbuli darávord." *(No matter what I said, he produced a lame excuse).*
"Xub bámbuli behew zad." *(He played a very good (practical) trick on him. Not a joke)*
"Havá emruz hamaw bámbul dar miyáre." *(It is very changeable weather today.)*
"Bámbul" *conveys a sense of dishonest, nonacceptable excuse or trick.*
*[etymology: cf* अंगुर *bhangura (Sanskrit): (adj) 1- changeful, variable [2- crooked, bent 3- fraudulent, dishonest, crafty.]*

9

## BÁREKALLÁ = BÁRIKALLÁ

*Used only as an exclamation, conveying a sense similar to "bravo!", or "well-done!"*

"In dáru ro boxor, pesar ján, áre bárikallá!" *(Take this medicine, my son, bravo! Here you go!")*

*etymology: Directly derived from the "Arabic" "tabárak Alláh".*

## BÁR-O-BANDIL

*See* "bandil".

## BEIQULE

*(An empty formidable place)*

"Xáneaw beiqule ast." *(His house is an empty formidable place.)*

"Biyábán e beiqule" *(Wasteland; formidable desert)*

[*etymology*: beiq-ul-e *cf* "beiq" विकट vikát *(1- formidable, frightful, horrible, dreadful 2- fierce, savage 3- great, large, broad, spacious, wide 4- proud.) Also compare with* "biq".]

## BELBEWU = VELVEWU

"Kár e má saxt belbewust." *(Our work is badly confused or our business is in chaos.)*

"Nemiduni ce belbewuyi wod!" *(You can't imagine the chaos.)*

"Hame já belbewu o valvá bud." *(Everywhere, there was chaos and turmoil.)*

[*etymology: In contrast to what appears in FM p.565,* (belbewu = behel bewou! *Leave, and go!*)]

"belbewu" *is derived in the following fashion:*

[bel-, = vel-, = váhel < váhewtan, váhelidan. *(leave alone; abandon; give up)*]

## BESSE

"Uno besse!" *(Look at him!)*

"Káko sey kon!" (Wirázi) *(Shirazi dialect) (Look, brother!)*

"Seyl kardan" *(Shirazi dialect) (to watch, pay attection)*

"seyl kede." (Lori ye Kuháni) *(to look, watch)*

[*etymology*: besse = be-, *(verbal prefix)* + se. *"Se" has nothing to do with the Arabic* "seir).

"se" < sah-ist-an (Pahlavi) *(to seem; pay attention)* ("Hakar wmáh baqán sahet" (Pahlavi), *"If His Majesty pays attention to...."*)(BF. P.494)]

## BETAMARG! TAMARGIDAN

"Betamarg" *is an imperative form of the verb* "tamargidan". *(To sit or lie down, and keep quiet and still).  Thus,* "Bacce ye toxs, begir betamarg!" *(Oh! You hyperactive and restless child, sit down, and keep quiet!)*
[*etymology: omit* "be-" *(verbal particle):* tamarg? 1- tam ≡ dam दम् *dam (Sanskrit)(to be tamed, to be subdued, or restrained,  to be calm or tranquil);* -arg√?;
*or:* 2-ta-marg-idan, tamarg < de-, *(repeatedly-); marg: ?*]

## BEW

*This word is almost exclusively used in combination with* "xow" *as* "xow-o-bew".
"Newastim o xow-o-bew kardim." *"We sat down and talked about things sweet (good), and all things bad." (All things in life that we had experienced.")*
[*etymology and semantic reconstruction:* "bew < (Pahlavi) *(1-pain, 2-grief, 3-harm, injury)*
bew ≡ viw: *primary concept: bitter, anything bitter* ≠ "xow" *(sweet), cf.* áb e xow = áb e wirin.
viw = bew, *(aconitum) (a very bitter poisonous plant root)*
bew-á z = *1-therapy, therapeutics, 2-therapeutic, 3-medicine, cure*
bew-áz-ih *(Pahlavi) (1-medicine – the art of healing) (2-cure)*
cf. pezewk *(physician)*
viw *(Pahlavi) (1- bile, 2- venom, 3- poison, toxin)*
cf. vew-gun, *see* viw.]

## BEZANG

*Only used as* "guw bezang": "Hame wab guw bezang budam." *(I waited expectantly, all night.)*
"bezang", "bazang", "baźang": *(1- key, house key, 2- door bell, 3- knocker of the door)*

## BEZANGÁH

"Sar e bezangáh ámad." *(He came at the very crucial moment.")(He arrived in time (for...)*
"Sar e bezangáh goft." *(He said at the very proper time.)*

"bezangáh": *A place where highway robbers lurk. Figuratively crucial point.* *(FM)*
[*author's view*: bezan-gáh, gáh = *time, place*; bezan = bazan *cf* vijin, gozin *(selected, choice, exclusive). Thus, at the very choice moment or place".*]

# BIGODÁR
"Bigodár" *is almost exclusively used as,* "bigodár be áb zadan." *(To enter a body of water (river, sea etc) on horse-back or on foot, not knowing exactly the dangers of the depth, and what lies ahead.)*
["Bigodár be áb zad." *(He took a great risk.)*]
[*etymology*: bi-godár: bi-, *privative prefix.* godár: *ford, a shallow place in a body of water where a crossing can be made.* godár < gozawtan, gozar < vitartan *(Pahlavi)(to cross, pass)* < vi-tar *(Avest)(BF, BQM)*]

# BIJ-BIJ
*This word is used only during Nouruz Holidays, when similar to Easter in the west, eggs are colored and decorated. The children may play* "bij-bij", *in which each contender holds an egg on end, in her/his hand and tries to crack the opponent's egg by tapping her/his egg on the opponent's egg.*
"Biyá, bij-bij bázi konim." *(Come, let's play* "bij-bij")
[*etymology*: bij < vij *(Pahlavi)*: seed, race, dynasty. *(BF. p.596)*
बीजं *bijan (Sanskrit): seed, grain, germ, element.*
Irán vij: *the origin of the Iranian people.*]

# BILÁX, BILAX
*This word is used as an exclamatory remark. It is used when somebody requests something illogical, or such in excess of what seems to be fair or just. In response one would answer* "bilax!" *or* biláx. *It is commonly associated with a fist and an upturned thumb. The exclamation and the gesture with the hand, make the other individual understand* "come on! Your position or request is hopeless, and I would not give a damn to it!"
[*etymology*: bilax → bil-ax,
"bil" = bel, = vel < vá-helidan, váhewtan: *To give up, abandon, leave alone.*
"ax", = áx = < axv' *(Pahlavi) (1- lord, master 2- life, existence 3- world 4- intellect, conscience)*
*semantic reconstructin: Axv is present in*: farrox, bestáx, gostáx, dmaq, dorváx, ostoxán, duzax, biq]

## BINE

"Bine" *(Bath-house ante chamber) is a small room where one takes off one's clothes, before entering a bath for taking a bath. "Bine" is classically built with one exit and one door opening into the bath-house. There is a platform where one sits, rests, and leaves her/his clothing.*
"Raft sar e bine newast." "*(He went and sat in the "bine"). The word is used either alone or as shown above, combined with "sar".*
[*etymology*: √?; bine]

## BIPIR

"Pir e már o darávord." (*He really gave us a hard time.*)
"Sarmá ye bipiri bud." (*It was awfully cold.*)
"Pir e kasi ra´darávardan" = *to give somebody really a hard time, to make someone suffer badly.* "Bipir" *as an adjective, means "awful", "extremely hard", anything causing suffering".*
[*etymology*:
"pir = pedar, (*father*) cf per (*Gilani*)(*father*) < pitrá (*Sanskrit*)
"bipir" = bipedar (*fatherless*) (*of very bad nature*)
"Pir e kasi rá darávardan" = "Pedar e kasi rá darávardan." (*to give somebody a very hard time.*)
*In both cases "pir" is exactly "pedar". It has nothing to do with "pir" meaning "old", In some literary works, "pir" preferably signifies "father" rather than "old", e.g.:*
"Pir e má goft xatá bar qalam e son-, naraft
                           Áfarin bar nazar e pák e xatápuwaw bád!" (Háfez)]

## BIQ

*Stupid-ignorant, uninformed.*
"Yáru pák biq-e!" (*He is totally ignorant!*)
[*etymology*: biq = bix; bi-q = bi-x: bi-, *without, -less (privative prefix)*
-q = -x < axv́: *mind, intelligence. Thus*: biq = *without intelligence, stupid.*
*Semantic reconstruction: Cf* an-axv *(Pahlavi)(lordless)(BF p.75), also compare* "beiqule".]

## BISÁR

"Bisár" *is the short or colloquial form of* "bástár" *or* "bistár". *Almost always used as* "bisár kas" *synonymous with* "folán kas", *"A so-and-so", "a certain person".*

"Bisár kas goft boro!" *"A so-and-so, said "go!"" "The classic form of* "bástár o bistár" *(A so-and-so) is not used in slang Persian.*

[*etymology*: bisár = bistár; bisár = bi-star

bi-, vi-, *(separate, different, other)*

star-, *to spread. cf* gostar, bestar, setáre

*thus,* "bistár" *"other, some other".*]

## BIX

*root, radix*

"bix" *can be used synonymous with* "riwe" *or* "bon".

"Deraxt rá az bix kand." *"He uproóted the tree."*

"bix e in giyáh wirin ast." *"The root of this plant is sweet."*

[*etymology*: "bix" *cf* वीजं *vijan (Sanskrit)(seed, origin, source),*

*also see* "bij-bij".]

## BOL

"Bol" *is used only in the form of* "bol gereftan" *and* "bol dádan." *Literally "to catch a* <u>bol</u>*" and "to give a* <u>bol</u>*", respectively. These expressions are primarily used in a game of tipcat, where a small bar of wood is struck with a bat and other players try to catch this small stick (which is called* "dolak"*), while flying in the air. Thus any player who can catch a flying* "dolak", *is said to have a* "bol gereft", *and any player, who has thus given the opportunity of winning to the other player, is said to have given a* "bol dáde". *As the opportunity is symbolized as a flying object, which is caught in the air,* "bol" *is used figuratively.*

[*etymology*: "bol" = "vol": *cf* "vol" *(French) = flight,* volatile < volare *(Latin) "to fly". Also* "voleur" *(French) = burglar, from the same root.*

*cf* वर्वरा *várvárá (Sanskrit)(A sort of fly).*]

## BOQ

"boq kardan" *(to put on a depressed, morose or solemn facies or air)" (to look sad).*

"Ci wode bázam boq kardi?" *"What's wrong, you look sad or moody again?"*

[*etymology and semantic reconstruction*: "boq" *cf* "baq": bagha (Avestá) *portion, share*, "bag" (Avestá) *to apportion, to distribute*; baxtan, baxw (Pahlavi) *to apportion, to distribute. (BQM p.288) (MK p.17).* "Baq" *(God, Lord) is from the same root of* "bag". *Also note that all are derived from the Sanskrit word*: "Bhaga", "bhagván" भगवान्. *Aslo cf.* "bay", "beyg", "bak" (*All Turkish*), *meaning "Lord", "Master. Also cf* "Ozbak" "Uzbak". *As "God" is characterized by a solemn facies, the slang Persian term* "boq kardan", *means, "to put on a solemn facies, as the Gods". Also cf the slang term* "gonde-bak" (*someone who is of mature age, but who does immature things, or has childish manners.*)] *cf* natarbuq.

## BUQ E SAG

(*Until very late in night*)
"Tá buq e sag naxábid." (*He did not go to bed until very late in night.*)
"buq e sag" *literally: until the dogs start barking, late in night.*
[buq < √ vac *(Avest)(to sing)*; vaocat *(Avest)(to speak)*; √ vác *(Sanskrit)(word, sound, talk, speech). Also these words are of the same root*: váźe (*word*); vátan (*to speak*); vájidan (*to speak*) (*to say*); váj (*prayer*); báź (*prayer*); váź (*prayer*). *Also note* vaq, vaq-vaq *(barking).*
*Also the following words derive from the same root*: voix *(French)(voice)*; voice *(English)*; vox (*Latin*)]

## BUR

1- *As and adjective* "bur" *means "blond".* "doxtar e mu bur", *"A girl with blond hair".* "Muw o bur kard." *"she dyed her hair blond".*
2- *But* "bur wodan": "Ámad wirini boxore, dar e quti ro báz kard, hicci tuw nabud, bur wod." *"He wanted to take a piece of cake, he opened the box, but the box was empty, he was badly disappointed."* "Bad juri burew kardam". *"I disappointed him very badly." "I embarrassed him very rudely."*

"bur": *a bay horse, or fox. reddish-brown.*
[*etymology*: "Bur" *in* "bur wodan" *or* "bur kardan" *is thought to be derived from the reddish color, as explained above for the hair. When somebody is embarrassed he/she blushes, therefore the use of* "bur." *"Old paper" may turn* "bur" *and cloth partially scorched may turn* "bur". *Again both become yellowish brown, not "red" or "rosy". Cf* "bavra" (*Avest*) *red; bur (Pahlavi),*

bur *(Tabari)(yellow)(BQM p.314).  Also cf* बभ्रु *babhru (Sanskrit) = deep brown, reddish brown.*]

1- Grundriss der iranischen Philologie: w. Geiger, E. Kuhn, 1895-1901

# C

**CAK**

"Cak" *a slap on the face or cheek.* "Cak zadan", *to give someone a slap on the cheek.* "Cak xordan", *to be given a slap on the cheek.* "Cak" *is synonymous with* "kewide" *and* "sili". *Also,* "sili zadan", "sili xordan", "kewide zadan", "kewide xordan".
*etymology*: ?

**CAK O CIL**

"Cak o cil" *is synonymous with* "cak o cune". *Mostly used as*: Áb az cak o cilew sarázir wod!" *"His mouth watered profusely (as a sign or craving for something at the time of seeing desirable things or an attractive girl or woman)".*
[*etymology*: "cak" *head, cf* cakád. *See* "cak o cune"
"cil" *cf* cune, = cáne *(chin). Cf* cena (Lori)*(chin).*]

**CAK O CUNE**

"Cak o cunaw xord wod." *"His head and chin were smashed."*
"Zad cak o cunaw o xurd kard." *"He beat him and smashed his head and chin."*
"Áb az cak o cunaw sarázir wod." *"He started drooling profusely (a sign of craving for something.)"*
"Cak o cune zadan": *to talk much, to talk idly; to talk much in order to bargain, while purchasing something.*
"Xeyli cak o cune zad ammá be jáyi naresid." *"He bargained a lot but in vain."*
[*etymology*: "cak", *head, vertex of the head. Cf* "cakád" *(vertex),* "cakát" (Pahlavi) = *peak, summit, top.*]

**CALQUZ**

*This pejorative word is used as a substantive, referring usually to someone, signifying a man of low caliber, and low social status, and usually physically small and unattractive.*

"Martike ye calquz ámade xástegári ye doxtar e kadxodá." *"The despicable man is asking for the hand of the village chief's daughter."*
*etymology:* "Calquz" *is described as meaning,* "bird's dropping, *however, this meaning has nothing to do with the slang word used above, meaning* "a man of short stature, and low caliber."
"calquz = cal-quz: "cal" ≡ wal, *cf.* wal-vár, wal-ang, wal-ite, "wal" = *leg.*
"quz" *cf.* kuź, guź, = *curved, and deformed legs, as the rickety patients, with genu varum or genu valgum, thus* "calquz" *somebody (of poor figure) with crooked legs.*
[*semantic reconstruction:* guź= *convex, bent, cf* quz, kuz, kuź, kuze, kez (kardan), quze, anquze, gouz, jouz, quzak.]

## CAMUW

*This term basically refers to a wild unruly horse, mule or draft animal. Also figuratively used, when referring to individuals who are unruly and restive.*
"Pesar e camuwi dáre." *"He has a very unruly, undisciplined son."* *The word is a substantive, thus it can be used both as an adjective, and a noun.*
[*etymology:* camuw = ca-muw: ca-, ≡ gáv, gou, gá-,: muw = miw: *thus,* "camuw" ≡ gá-miw, = gáv-miw. *A bison, or buffalo, a symbol of strength and unruliness.*]

## CANTE

"Cante", *a satchel, a bag. Usually used as:* "cizi dar cante nadáre." = "Cantaw xáliye." *"His bag is empty." = "He does not know much."* "Cantaw por-e." *"His bag is full."* *He knows a lot.*
[*etymology:* cante = cant-e; *cf* शान्पुट:: *wanputáh (Sanskrit) = a bag. cf* "cán" *in* "cáncu" (Gilaki) = *Two wicker baskets, suspended at the two ends of a wooden bar, carried on the shoulders.* "cán-cu" = cán = *bag, and* cu = cub = *stick, rod.*]

## CAPOU

*Almost always used with the verbs* "kardan" *or* "wodan": "capou kardan" *"to plunder, to loot",* and "capou wodan" *"To be plundered or looted."*
"Ámadan xunaw o capou kardan." *"They came and plundered his house."*
*etymology:* "capou" < "capávol". "capávol" *(Turkish) = plunder, plundering.* (*BQM p.620*). [?]

## CAPPE

"Cappe" *is almost always used with* "kardan" *or* "wodan", *meaning "to overturn" (vt), and "to capsize" (vi).*

"Máwin cappe wod." *"The car turned over."*

"Máwin o cappe kardan!" *"They turned the car over."*

*etymology*: cappe = capp-e? < cap = *left, reverse, in the opposite direction.*

## CARAND, CARAND O PARAND

*Almost synonymous with* "cart o part", "cert; cert o pert".

"Carand mige." = "Cart mige." *"He says nonsense."*

"Cart o part mige" = "Carand o parand mige." *"He says nonsense."*

[*etymology*: cart = car-t, carand = car-and: "-t", *and* "-and", (*suffixes*); "car" *cf* चर् *car (Sanskrit): to go about, wander, roam.*

"parand = par-and; "-and" (*suffix*); *see* "part".

## CART; CERT

*Also see* "carand"

*"This word is usually use in combination shown below:*

"Cart o part", "cert o pert". *"idle talk, nonsense"*

"Cart o part mige." *"He says nonsense."*

*etymology: See* "carand".

## CÁK

*a tear, cut, slit*

"Dastew cák xord." *"His hand was slit open."*

"In o cák bede!" *"Cut this asunder!", "slit this."*

*etymology: See* "cál".

## CÁKER

*"This term is used almost always as a noun, rarely as an adjective, meaning "an obedient, sincere servant.*

"Áqá, má cáker e womá-yim." *"Sir, I am your obedient servant."*

[*etymology*: cá-ker-; *cf* cá-kudan *(Gilaki)(to fix, put right; to cure; to execute efficiently)*: kudan = kardan, cá √?: *Thus* cáker *(literally: Somebody who does a good job.)*]

## CÁL

"Cál" *means a cavity, a pit.*

"Mixande, loppew cál miyofte." *"When she smiles, she has dimples on her cheeks."*

"Mizani cewm o cálet o kur mikoni." *"You may hit your eye, and (other) cavities, and you may blind yourself."*

[*etymology and semantic reconstruction: cf* cáh, *a well;* cál; cál-e, *a pit, cavity;* cák, *a split, crack, slit. cf* "cát' (Avest), *a well*

शकलीभू *wákálibhu, a split (Sanskrit)*

छो *cho,* छात *chátá (Sanskrit) = to cut asunder.*]

## CÁQ O CELLE

"Cáq" *means "fat".* "Celle" *used in this context, is not used alone.*

"Cáq o celle" *combined, means, "plump, well-fed, and rotund".*

"Do gusfand e cáq o celle ávordan." *"They brought two well-fed, and plump sheep." "Two well-fed, and plump sheep were brought forth."*

*etymology:* √?

## CÁRQAD

*This word means a square or oblong headdress used by women to cover hairs.*

"Cárqad be sarew kard o raft." *"She wore her headdress and left."*

*etymology:* √?

## CEFT

*a hasp, latch.*

*This is the word specific for a latch consisting of a plate with a hook. The hook is inserted into a snare-like device, and a lock is put on the hook.* "Dar o ceft kon!" *"Lock the door with a latch."*

[*etymology:* युगः *yugáh (Sanskrit), a yoke:* yuxta *(Avest) (BQM p.647)*

*Semantic reconstruction:* "Yugáh", *basic concept, to unite, to attach two things together. Cf* sef-t, jof-t, yuq, joq, *yoga,* zoft (?), sanjáq, sanjáf = sejáf.]

## CEL

*See* "xol-o-cel".

"Doxtare cel-e!" *"That girl is loose in character."*

"Doxtare xol o cel-e." *"That girl is of low intelligence and loose in character."*

*[etymology: Cf* चिल्ल *cilla, (Sanskrit)(1- to be or become loose or slack. 2- to act wantonly). In contrast to what appears in the Persian dictionaries "cel" does not mean "idiot or stupid" (FM, p.1304), because there is no need to repeat the word in "xol", which means "idiot". I believe as the writers of the dictionaries were not critical in their evaluation of the meanings of the words, they assumed "cel" to be synonymous with "xol". (also see BQM) "Cel" means somebody who acts wantonly. also col ≡ wol (slack, thus lacking ambition or purpose.)]*

## CELOU

*white rinsed pilaf.*
"celo xorew" *"White cooked rice and stew"*
"Celou" *is a rice pilaf, which its starch is rinsed with copious amounts of water during preparation. This is in contrast to* "kate", *which is not rinsed with water, during preparation.*
[*etymology*: celou = cel-ou; cel = wal = cal, शालि:: *wálih (Sanskrit) = rice.*
*Cf* wal-tuk, *rough rice, paddy*; caltuk = *paddy*; wáli, wálizár = *rice-field.*
ou = áb *(=water).* "wole-zard", "wol-e" < wálih *(rice);* wole-qalam-kár]

## CERT

*See* "cart".

## CEWM O CÁL

*See* "cál".

## COLÁQ

"Coláq" *means, lame, paralyzed, crippled.*
"Páw coláq-e." *"His leg is lame or paralyzed."*
"Dastew coláq-e." *"His arm is either paralyzed or stiffened due to joint or muscle disease, so that he cannot use it effectively."*
"Coláq" *is used when for any reason one cannot use a limb. The disease may be in the in the nervous system (i.e. paralysis), in the muscular system, or in the joints.*
[*etymology*: coláq = √? col-áq: *cf.* col, wol, wal (*leg*); walang; walang-taxt e; walite, walvár + áq = ák *(disease, flaw, defect). Thus* coláq: *defective leg.*]

21

## COLMAN

"barádarew colman-e." *"His brother is an incompetent, and infirm man in character and action." The term is used to depreciate a person in ambition and purpose.*
[*etymology*: colman = col-man: "col"; xol; man = manew = *character, cf* "bahman", "vohuman", "dowman", "sepantámana", "human". *Thus shiftless, lacking ambition, purpose and resourcefulness.*]

## COLOFTI

*Also see* "Dast o pá colofti."
"Colofti" *is almost exclusively used as* "dast o pá colofti", *referring to somebody whose arms and legs move not in coordination, thus being awkward in movements, falling or dropping things with quite simple movements.*
"Xeyli dast o pá colofti-ye." *"He is very awkward, and thus incompetent."*
[*etymology*: colofti = col-oft-i: col, *see* cel, wol,: oft, *cf* oftádan, पत् *pát (Sanskrit) to fall*; oft-i; colofti: *falling limp, or slack. Also* "cafte, caftidan" "cafte" = *curved, crooked, cf* "cap"]

## CONDAK = conbak (*squatting, to squat*)

"Condak zadan" *is synonymous with* "qond zadan", *see* "qond".
"Condak zade ye guwe neweste." *"He pulled his arms and legs together, and squatted in a corner."*
*etymology*: condak = cond-ak, *see* "qond".

## COQOLI

*This term is used when somebody bears tales against somebody else.* "Coqoli kardan az kasi." *is used when someone reports news about somebody and expands on his shortcomings or bad aspects, in order to put him in disfavor and therefore make him deserve punishment or reprimand.*
"Rafte coqoli ye man o be pedaram karde." *"He has reported news about me to my father, with malicious intentions."*
[*etymology*: √?: *cf* cart, *cf* żakidan, *to grumble or complain in low voice. Cf* zeq, zeq zadan (*to nag*); żakidan. coqoli = coq-ol-i; *cf* "coq", *and* "żak" "coqol" *tale bearer (BQM p.645).*]

## CORDE

*Almost always used as* "siyáh corde" *or* "siyah corde", *meaning "of dark complexion".*
*The term is applied to people with very dark facial complexion, most of the time also slightly wrinkled.* "Mard e siyah cordeyi az xáne birun ámad." "A dark-complexioned man came out of the house."
[*etymology*: corde = cord-e; *cf* carze (? = cord) = *body and facial skin (BQM P.631, 632). Cf.* जरायु *cáráyu (Sanskrit): 1-The slough or cast-off skin of a serpent. 2- The outer skin of the embryo.*]

## CORT

"*Almost always used as* "cort zadan" "*to take a cat nap*", *or* "*to take a nap*". *A short sleep, either, lying or in sitting position, to snooze.*
"Bezár ye corti bazanam." "*Let me take a nap.*"
*etymology: ?*

## COSÁN-FESÁN

"Cosán-fesán" *is a depreciative term for make-up and cosmetics, as well as dressing oneself up.* "Cosán-fesán o besse!" "*Hey look! Such a make-up!*"
"Emruz xeyli cosán-fesán kardi, ce xabar-e mage?" "*Today you've put on a lot of make-up and you have dressed up smartly, what's up?*" *The term can be used for women and men.*
[*etymology*: Cosán-fesán *clearly derived from* "cos" *and* "fes" *respectively. See* "cos", "fes", *and* "cos-o-fes". –án, *suffix, forming substantive, eg* "Juyán", *and* "puyán".]

## COSI

"Cosi" *almost always used with* "ámadan", *thus* "cosi ámadan" *means* "*To brag about something and to act ostentatiously*". "Cosi nayá!" "*Don't brag! Don't show off!*". "Cerá cosi miyáy(i)?" "*Why do you brag and show off?*"
"Cos" *is a noiseless gas passed from the anus.* "Cosi" *is most probably related with* "cos". "Cos" *is also a pejorative and depreciative term, symbolically and figuratively related with other uses of this term. Thus* "cos" *means, meager, meagerness, a small amount, incompetent, of low caliber, small size, etc.* "Ye cos guwt." "*A small piece of meat.*" "Mardeke ye cos." "*Small, incompetent, despicable man.*"
*etymology: √?*

23

## COS O FES

"Cos o fes" *means "a meager amount", "barely sufficient".* "Ye omri bá cos-o-fes zendegi kard." *"He lived a life with meager income."* "Bá in cos-o-fesá kár dorost nemiwe." *"With this meager (amount of money) one cannot hope any improvement in the business."*
[*etymology*: "cos", *see* "cos".
"Fes": *is an onomatopoeic word, referring to the hissing sound of an emitting gas from an aperture.*]

## COSENE

*See* "cosone".

## COSONE = COSENE

"Cosone" *or* "cosene" *literally means a* "beetle", *a* "dung beetle". *This word is used to refer to an individual who interferes with a job requiring greater skill or strength. The term is depreciative.* "Pesare ye cosene das az saram bar nemidáwt." *"The despicable lad, did not leave me alone."*
[*etymology*: cosone = cosene cos-en-e = cos-in-e, *suffix* = -a, -ak; -en = -in, *adjective forming suffix, eg.* "jovin" *"made of barley",* "cubin" *"made of wood" and* "cosen = cosin": *"made of* "cos". *Thus anything or anybody or creature of small stature, strength and ability. Also see* "cosi".]

# D

**DABANG**

"Martike ye dabang, engár az powt e kuh umade." *"The crazy, ignorant man, behaves in such a way, as though he comes from behind the mountains, thus not exposed to knowledge, and civilization."* "Dabang" is also used to signify a state of dizziness, confusion and altered state of mind.
[etymology: √?: *Primary concept, compatible with*: "mang" *and* "bang" (*henbane hashish, cannabis, hemp".* Cf भंगा *bhángá (Sanskrit)(hemp, an intoxicating drink prepared from hemp.)*]

**DAGANAK**

*This is used only as* "bá daganak", "bá daganak + *verb*" *"to do something by lots of force, urging and stimulation." "If somebody is not willing to do something, and eventually gets to do it by considerable cajoling and pushing, one would say* "bá daganak ....", *thus* "Bá daganak dars mixune." *"He studies only by force."* "Bá daganak mire xodew o miwure." *"He takes a bath only after being pushed to do so."*
[etymology: daganak = dagan-ak: dagan, *cf* dahan, daganak, *cf* dahanak: *The mouthbit of a bridle.*]

**DAK O DANDE**

"Zad dak o dandaw o xurd kard." *"He beat him and smashed his head and ribs."* "Dak o dandaw wikast." *"His head and ribs were broken."*
[etymology: dak√?; dande = dand-e, dand, *cf* दंतः : dántáh *(a tooth, an elephant's tusk).* Cf dand, dande, dandán. *Any tooth-like projection.*]

**DAK O DIM**

"Zad dak o dimew o xurd kard.." *"He beat, and smashed his head and face."* "Zad tu dak o dimew." *"He beat up his head and face."*
etymology: dak √?;
dim: daeman-, (Avest)(*face*); dem (*Armenian*)(*face*); dem (*Kurdish*)(*face*); dim (*Gilaki*)(*face.*)(*BQM p.915*)]

## DAK O PUZ

"dak" = *head*, "puz" = *muzzle (pejorative chin).  Thus "dak o puz" = "head and mouth", "head and chin", figuratively "smartly dressed."* "Zad dak o puzew o xurd kard." *"He beat him up and broke his head and chin."* "Biyá bebin ce dak o puzi!" *"come and see, how dandy he has dressed up!"*
[*etymology*: dak √?
puz: puz (Pahlavi), *muzzle*,; puzak (Pahlavi) *muzzle*.
*cf.* पुंजि *punji (Sanskrit)(a heap, mass).*
*cf.* पुंजितः *punjitáh (Sanskrit)(1- pressed together, 2- heaped together.)*]

## DAK WODAN, DAK KARDAN

"Dak wod." *"He scurried away.", "He went away surreptitiously, without noise, thus attracting no attention."*
"Did havá pas-e, dak wod!" *"He foresaw a bad situation, thus he fled."*
"Xub dakew kardiyá!" *"You got rid of him very smartly!"*
"dak kardan" *"To make someone go away by asking him to do something, thus getting rid of him."* "Dakew kon!" *"Send him away and get rid of him!"*
[*etymology*: dak *cf* tak, takidan, *to run*. √ tak, tac *(to run)*("taka" *Avestan*) táxtan, tázidan = *to run (BQM p.503)*]

## DAM

1- "dam e…" *(close to, at…)*
   "Dam e marg". *"At the time of death."*
   "Dam e dar." *"Close to the door."*
2- dam = *mouth*; "Sage bowqáb o dam zad." *"The dog licked the dish."*
3- dam zadan *(1- to lick, see above.  2- to brag)*
4- "Hey az xodew dam mizane." *"He brags a lot about himself."*
5- dam = *the cutting edge.* "Hama ro az dam e tiq gozarund.": *"He killed everybody." Literally "He made everybody pass by the cutting edge of the sword."*
[*etymology*: "dam" *(close to)*, "dam" *(mouth)*, and "dam" *(the cutting edge), all the apparently incongruous meanings can be tied together under the root of* "dam" *(to breathe, breath).  dham (Sanskrit), to breathe, to blow (BQM p.876)*]

## DAMARU

= domáru *(tailwise, tailward, caudad) (Prone position)* = damar.
"Damaru xábe tu áftáb." *"He is lying prone in the sunlight."*

[*etymology*: damaru = dama-ru, *cf* domá-ru, dombáru, donbáru.
*cf* bi-run, vá-run, vá-ru, da(r)-run = darun, anda(r)-run, andarun, fará-run.
run = ru; *direction, side, -ward*. Damaru = *dama-run. *Thus "damaru" means,*
*"dama"-, wise, -wise or "dama-" ward, or towards* dama. + domb, donb.]
[*also cf.* nehá-vand, nehá-, *front, forward*; damá-vand,: damá-, = dombá-,
donbá-, *behind, back, tail (Kárvand e Kasravi). Thus*: dama-ru = *dombá-ru;
*lying in such a way, so that the tail, or back part is directed upward. "run" =*
*"ru", is not related to "ru", "ruy" (face).*
*compare*: "Ye doxtar e zibá ye áftábru" *"A beautiful girl, with a sun-like face."*
(ru = ruy = *face*)
"In otáq áftábru-s." *"This room looks toward the sun." "It is "sun-ward". (ru*
= run = *direction, side, -ward*)
"damaru" = "domáru" *is antonym of* "setán". *"Setán" is erroneously spelled as*
*"siyán" (Due to the inadequacy of the Arabic alphabet, imposed on Persian).*
*Thus, "Setán xoftan" (not "siyán xoftan") to lie in supine position.*]

# DAMAQ

"Zad tu zoqqew, pák damaq wod." *"He was rebuked or discouraged very*
*rudely, and thus he became depressed."*
[*etymology*: damaq = dam-aq = *tam-axv.
"dam" *cf* tam (Pahlavi) = *tom, darkness.*
"aq" = axv (Pahlavi*) (1- lord, 2- existence, essence of life, 2- world, 4-*
*intelligence, conscience, thought) (BF p.543) thus, "dam-aq" = dark mood,*
*sad. also cf* duzax, farrox, bestáx, gostáx, áxund,? barzax.]

# DAND

*Only used as* "Dandet narm." (*Your ribs, beaten up and smashed, and softened*
*in consistency) meaning that you deserved the punishment or consequences of*
*what you did. "Therefore it is said to someone, who has received the bad*
*consequences of an unwise action.*
[*etymology*: "dand" = *rib, cf* dande. dandán, दंतः *dántáh (tooth). See*: "dak o
dande".]

# DANG O FANG

*This word is used as a noun, and it refers to anything or any work or process*
*which is complicated and is fraught with many delicate steps.*

"Kár kardan e bá in carx xeyli dang o fang dáre." *"Working with this machine is very complicated."*

"Ceqad dang o fang dári!" *(Dealing with you is difficult)* or *"You take so much time to get ready for doing something or going somewhere."*

[*etymology*: dang, *cf* danghah-, *(Avest)(= skill, aptitude). dansas (Sanskrit)* √ *dens (Walde-Pokorny, p.201)* √ *dens + fang, fang ≡ vang, cf vanghu (Avest)(good, fine), thus: "dang o fang", something needing good skill and aptitude.*]

## DAQDAQE

"In ke dige daqdaqe nadáre." *"This work is easy, because there is nobody to trouble one, or to intervene."*

"Xub bi daqdaqe cand sáli zendegi kardihá!" *"Good for you! You lived several years without any intervention or trouble."*

*etymology*: daqdaqe < *Arabic* "daqdaqe" *(1- ticking, 2- bruising, 3-fear)*

## DARAK

"Be darak!" *"Hell with you!" or "Hell with it!"*

"Be darak ke gom wod." *"Now that it is lost, hell with it!"*

*etymology*: darak < *Arabic (the bottom of anything deep; to fall.)*

## DAST O PÁ COLOFTI

"Doxtare ye dast-o-pá colofti, zad kása ro wikund."

*"The clumsy, awkward girl, broke the bowl."*

*etymology: see "xol-o-cel", "cel" & "wol".*

## DAXOU

"Daxou ro xabar konin!" *"Summon the village elderman!" The "village elderman" is called "daxou" (a form of "dehxodá") in Qazvin, and its province.*

*"Daxou" is renown for his stupidity, especially in judgment or solving problems. Thus "When "Daxou" is summoned", one alludes to the stupidity of the individual in question.*

[*etymology*: "daxou" = "dehxodá": deh = dih = *village*, xou = xodá = *lord. Thus "daxou = dehxodá = the village headman or elder.*]

28

## DAYYUS

*This pejorative word is used when referring to a man (not a woman), who is of mediocre character, and without honor or self-esteem.   Specifically a cuckold, whose wife may be infidel to him, but he would not mind.*
"Martike ye dayyus" *"The cuckold!"*
*etymology: < Arabic.*

## DÁDÁW; DÁW

*This word means "a brother", "buddy"* "Dáw kojá budi?"  *"Hey brother, where were you?"*  "Dádáwam bá ábjim raftan bázár."  *"My brother went to bazaar with my sister."*
dáw: *Shortened form of* "dádáw". "Dádár" dádáw *has a hidden meaning of endearment, kindness, whereas* "dáw" *is used by individuals who are hefty with bullying manners.*
Dáw *can be used as a title for men, eg* "Dáw Ali" *(Brother Ali, Mr. Ali)*
[*etymology:* dá-w; -w *archaic suffix* dá-, *and* dada, *cf* dá- *(mother);* dáyi *(maternal uncle)(related e mother);* dáw *and* dádáw, *(men sharing the same mother). A sign of kindness, and honoring the person addressed.*]

## DE

"De" *is probably a particle, or interjection used as:*
1- *A sign of interjection, to show surprise.* "Pedarew mord" *"His father died."* "De?!" *"Do you really mean it?!"* "Lule tarekid!" *"The pipe burst!"* "De?!" *"Do you really mean it?"*
2- *A verbal particle.  In this context, it means repeatedly, very much.* "De bezan!" *"beat and beat!".* "De boxor!" *"Eat and eat!"* *"Eat as much as you want."* "De biyá!" *"There is no end to it!  It continues to come!"*
[*etymology: Cf* atiy (*Old Persian*); aiti (*Avest*); आति *áti (Sanskrit)*]

## DEBW

*This word is almost always used in conjunction with* "cáy"*(tea).  In this context it means "Too strong and thus bitter."* "Cáyiw debw-e." *"This tea is too strong and thus a little bitter."  Occasionally it is used to refer to individuals, meaning "complete" "to the utmost degree."* "Yáru debwe debw-e!" *"He is totally unaware of what's going on."  "He is absolutely stupid."*

29

*etymology:* "debw" *is probably derived from* "dabs" *(Arabic) (inspissated grape juice." "Thick grape juice) (It is quite common to replace* "s" *with* "w" *in Persian.)* "cáy e debw" *bears resemblance to syrupy grape juice.*

## DEILÁQ

*This is a substantive. It is used in reference to a person male or female (usually male) who is awkwardly tall in stature. It is pejorative and is thus used only in this sense, eg* "Martike ye deiláq na dars mixune na kár mikone!" *(The lanky man does neither study nor work!")* or *"Hey, deiláq, biyá injá!"* *(Come on here, you lanky man!)*

[*etymology and semantic reconstruction:* deil-áq: áq *is a suffix equivalent of* -ak, -a *and* deil *is derived from the same root as* "deráz" < √ dareqa, drájah *(Avest). Also from the same root, compare:* dir *(late),* dirand, dirine, *etc.*]

## DENJ

*This is an adjective, use only with nouns denoting places.*
"Guwe ye denji peydá kard o xábid." *"He found a quiet corner and slept."*
"Xunaw tu já ye denji-ye." *"His house is located in a very quiet and tranquil place."*
*etymology:* ?

## DEQQ

1- "Deqq kardan" *"to die with grief and sorrow."*, "Deqq kard." *"He died with extreme grief."*

2- "Deqq e del e kasi wodan" *"to be the cause of extreme grief for someone."* "In pesare ye bikáre, wode deqq e del e xuneváde." *"This good-for-nothing boy has become the source of extreme frustration for his family."*

3- "Deqqe deli dar ávardan" *"To take (unfair) revenge upon someone."* "deqqe deli" = *revenge.* "Cerá deqqe delit o sar e un dar miyári?" *"Why you take (unjust) revenge upon him?"*

[*etymology:* "deqq" *probably derived from Arabic* "deqq", *meaning consumption, tuberculosis, any disease causing emaciation, to be thin.*]

## DODUZE

*See* "duz".

## DOLONBE

*This term is applied to anybody or any part of the body which is fat and cushion-like in softness and consistency.* "Kunew dolonba-s." *"Her buttocks are fat, soft and cushion-like."*
[*etymology: See* "áblambu."
*Semantic reconstruction: cf.* dolombe, qolonbe, donbalán, domal, dom, damaru]

## DOMAL

"Domal" *is an abscess.* "Páw domal karde" = "Páw domal dar ávorde." *"He has developed an abscess on his foot."*
[*etymology: cf* dom-al; donb-al; domb-al; donb-al-án; *also see* "áblambu".
√ dum, domb (Pahlavi) (*a tail*). -al, *a suffix.*
*I suspect that* "domal" *has no relation with the Arabic* "domal" *and* "dommal", *meaning* "boil" *and* "imposthum." *Even if related, it may have its origin in Persian, rather than the reverse. Semantic structure leads me to this assumption.*]

## DONBALÁN

"Donbalán" *means* "a testis", "a testicle", *especially that of animals, and specifically that of a ram.* "Del o qolve o donbalán mixorim." *"We eat roasted heart, kidney and (sheep) testicle."* "Donbalán" *is also used to signify* "fleshy mushrooms". *The mushrooms bear close resemblance to the testis of ram, in color and consistency.*
[*etymology*: dombalán = domb-al-án;, √ dum, dom (Pahlavi) (*a tail*); -al, -án *are suffixes. See*; domal, damaru, áblambu.]

## DUDUL

*See* "dul".

## DUL

"Dul" *is the term used for prepubertal penis. One affectionate way of addressing sons is* "dudul talá" (*gold-penis*).
[*etymology and semantic reconstruction: cf.* dul; dudul; dor (*Lori dialect hanging; dangling*); cor (*penis*); kir (*adult penis*); *also cf* kol-oft; col (*penis*); *cf* गुरुguru *(Sanskrit);* gurvi गुर्वि *(Sanskrit).* gouru *(Avest)(1- heavy; weighty 2- great; large); Also cf* qol-, *as in* "qoldor", "qol-comáq", "qolve", "qolve-sang",

qul", "qul-tawan", "xar-", "xarcang", "xarpul", "xarzur" *(meaning "big", "great", "heavy"), and prefix* "qara-," *(big, great, grand)* qara-caman *(big pasture, note this is not a Turkish word),* "qara-dáq" *(big mountain),* "qara-márs" *(badly (greatly) defeated)*]

## DUZ

duz-o-kalak, doduze

"Duz" *is used in combination:*

1- "Duz-bázi": *this is a sort of game (like checkers) played by children.*

2- "Do-duze bázi kardan", *eg.* "Doduze bázi mikoni" *"You play in a clever manner, holding both ways open eg in a negotiation, so you could shift to either side when necessary."*

3- "Duz-o-kalak", "duz-o-kalak zadan": *To play tricks, to be deceptive in one's dealings.*

[*etymology: Cf* duz, dow-, doź: *Also cf* "doźxim", "dow-pil", "duz-ax", "dozd". daoz-, *(Avesta),* doź-, *(Ancient Iranian);* dow-, *(Pahlavi)(bad, evil, wicked). The above root is not compatible with* "duz-bázi".]

## DUZ O KALAK

*See* "duz".

# F

## FATT O FARÁVUN

"Fatt" *is always used in combination, shown above.* "fatt-o-farávun" *means* "extremely abundant", "luxurious". "Waráb o xorák fatt-o-farávun bud." "There was an extreme abundance of wine and food."
[*etymology*: fat(t), *also see* "pat-o-pahn". *cf* पत् pat *(Sanskrit): 1- to fall down, come down. 2- set, sink (below the horizon). 3- To cast oneself at, throw oneself down. 4- to come down as from heaven. As though bounty has come down from the heaven. Also cf* "pát".]

## FÁL

"Fál": *anything especially like berries, nuts, or edible things which are arranged in equal numbers and put separately in small groups. Suppose putting five pieces of walnuts together, this constitutes one* "fál" *of walnut.* "Gerdu ro fali cand midi?" "How much do you sell each "fál" of walnut?"
[*etymology*: fál *cf.* bár. √ bár *(Avest) (to take, carry);* √ भृ bhri *(Sanskrit) (to carry); also cf* वारः : váráh *(Sanskrit), a heap, quantity, a large number*]

## FERR O FERR, FER FER

"Ferr ferr az damáqew xun umad." "He bled profusely from his nose."
"Ferr-(o)-ferr minevise." "He writes fast and profusely."
"Fer fer kár mikone." "He works a lot." "He works fast."
[*etymology: cf* fer-, fereh-, = *very much, ultra.* "fereh gande pir" "An extremely old man or woman". "Fer", "fere" *and* "fereh" *are confused with* "far-," *(prefix). There are many examples in Persian and Pahlavi, in which, to my belief,* "far" *is used instead of* "fer-,", *meaning much, or ultra. This seems to be primarily due to inadequacy of the alphabet.* "freh" *(Pahlavi): many, numerous, much excessive;* "farahya-," *(Avest); cf* पृथु prithu *(Sanskrit) – copious, abundant, ample, large, great, numerous.*]

## FES

"Fessew darumad." "The whole thing went down the drain.", "It went bezerk." *This is used when something which started in a falsely glorious way, breaks down totally and ends in total failure."*

[*etymology: This is an onomatopoeic word, for the air emitting from any aperture making a hissing sound. Also see "cos-o-fes" and, "fis". Thus "fis" is synonymous with "air", "wind" or "puffed-up-ness". "Fisu" "conceited" is one who is "puffed up" with pride. "fes" is anything insignificant, or worthlessness similar to a noiseless fart.*]

## FESFES

"Fesfes" *is almost always used with* "kardan". "fesfes kardan" *"to do something very slowly." "to procrastinate." Thus:* "Cerá fesfes mikoni?" *"Why do you procrastinate?"*

"Fesfesu" *means one who procrastinates, or somebody who is slow in doing things.*

"Fesfesu-s!" *"He is a perfect picture of slow-motion!"*

*etymology: See* "cos-o-fes".

## FESQEL

*Also* "fesqeli", "fesqele".

"Fesqel", *and* "fesqeli" *are both substantives.* "Ye bacce ye fesqel(i) umad namáyew dád." *"A very little child came (on the stage) and performed."*

"Fesqeli biyá!" *"Come on you midget!" "The term is used for people who are of small stature (and usually smart.)*

[*etymology and semantic reconstruction:* fesqel = fesq-el; *cf* fesq; pewk; pewgel; pesk; few, fes, pew *derived from fawu-, (Avest)(small domestic animal)*+gel<

pewgel: *sheep dung; horse dung; donkey dung.*]

## FIN

"Fin kardan" – *to blow one's nose.* "Fin kon!" – *blow your nose!* – "fin fin nakon!" – *Don't sniff!.* "Finfinu"; *A term to signify people who speak through their nose and sniff frequently while talking.*

[*etymology:* "fin" *is* vin, bin, binil *probably of onomatopoeic origin.*]

## FIS

"Fis" *is almost always used in combination with* "kardan". "Fis kardan" *"to show undue or false pride"* "fis o efáde" *"putting on airs", "behaving in conceited way."* "Fis nakon!" *"Don't show false pride!",* "Ce fis o efádeyi!" *"Such a conceited manner!"*

34

*etymology: See "fes".*

## FOKOL

"Be sarew fokol zade." *"She is wearing a bow on her hair."*

"Ye áqá ye fokoli umad birun." *"A man with neck-tie or bowtie came out."*

"Áqá fokoli biyá injá!" *"Hey, you smartly-clothed guy, come here!"*

"Fokol-keráváti ro besse!" *"Look at the dandy man (with necktie or bowtie)!"*

*etymology: "Fokol" is derived from the French word "faux col" (false collar) tied to the body of a shirt.*

## FOLÁNI

*also "folán"*

"Foláni umad, beppá!" *"Be careful, he (a so-and-so) is coming!"*

"Folán ruz raft." *"He went away on a so-and-so day."*

"Goft folán ruz biyá." *"He told me to come on a so-and-so date."*

"Folán-folán wode" *"the cursed man!", Damn it!; Damned!*

"Folán folán wode, xiyál mikone noukarewam." *"The cursed man, thinks that I am his servant."*

*etymology: "folán", derived from Arabic "folán (an unknown or a certain person.)*

35

# G

## GAB

"gab zadan" *"to chat" "to chatter"*

"Gab nazan!" *"(Don't speak! Keep quiet! Don't chatter)*

"Newastim o gab(i) zadim" *"We sat down and talked (chatted)."*

[*etymology: cf gab, goftan, guy-, guv́-, (guyam, guyán).*

gaub-, *(Old Persian) is the root of* "goftan" *(to say, to tell)*

*(BQM p.1821); Also cf gob, gop (Celtic) = the mouth.*]

## GAS

"Dahanam gas wod." *(I ate something which was astringent), thus my mouth became acrid.*

"Sib e kál o beh gas-an." *"Unripe apple and quince are astringent."*

*etymology:?*

## GAT

gat = kat, *see* "kat-o-koloft"

## GAZAK

"Gazak dassew nade." *"Don't give him a handle.", "Don't say anything, or don't do anything, that could give him an opportunity to take the upper hand, and thus be in a superior or winning position."*

*etymology:* "gazak" *directly derives from* "gazlik" *1- the barber's razor 2- a pen-knife, with a curved blade. In FM p.3307,* "gazak" *is considered to be of the same origin as* "gazak" *(Tehráni, Damávandi) = time, turn. Semantically it is difficult to tie this meaning with* "gazak" *as used in slang Persian. Cf gazak, gazlik, gazidan, gaźdom = kaźdom, and gazitan (Pahlavi).*

## GÁLE

"Gále" *is used as an adjective and occasionally as a noun.* "Dahan o! gál-as!" *"Look at that mouth! It is very large!" (Like the opening of a burlap sack).*

"Dahan e gálat o beband!" *"Shut your big mouth."*

*Though most commonly used for "mouth", it may also refer to other large and loose things, thus "Pirhanew gál-as." "Her dress is very large and unshapely.", "Her dress is like a sack."*
*etymology: Cf* gále, gevál *(Mázandaráni),* gál, guál *(Mázandaráni), also cf* gále, qár *(a cave).*

## GEZ RAFTAN

"Bá pesare gez miraft." *"He was fondling the young boy."*
"Gez narou!" *"Don't mess with him!"*
*This term denotes a behavior by a man towards a boy suggestive of either pedophilia or active male homosexuality.*
*etymology: ?*

## GIJ

*Dizzy, confused. "go-gije."; "gij o vij": very confused.*
"gij" *is a substantive. It means dizzy and confused, perplexed.*
"Pák gij wodam." *"I was totally confused."*
"Bábá gij wode." *"The guy is totally confused."*
*etymology: See "gogije".*

## GIS

*This word is used singular or plural, to signify long hair.*
"Gisát o bebáf." *(plural),* "Giset o bebáf ." *(singular) "Braid your hair."*
"Haf pesar e kákol zari yo haf doxtar e gis golabatun." *"Seven sons with blond hair and seven daughters with gold-braided hair."*
[*etymology:* gis < gaesa *(Avest),* ges *(Pahlavi)(BQM P.1869) cf.* bádqeis, vát-gis *(Pahlavi),* vaiti-gaesa *(Avest)(BF p.587)* vat-gis *(Armenian)*]

## GOGIJEH

"Go-gije gereftan" *to be extremely confused, so that one does not know what to do. To be perplexed. To move around not knowing what to do.*
"Cerá go-gije gerefti?" *"Why you are so badly confused?"*
[*etymology:* go-gije: *cf Jig (English): Old French* gigue *< Old High German* gigan. *German dialect:* geigen, *to move back and forth. German:* Geige, *a fiddle. Base of Dannish gig: spinning top. English gig: carriage, boat, top. Base of both: erratic movement. Indo-European base:* ghei: *to yawn, split, open.*

*The first part*: "go-", *is not related with* "goh" *"feces." (folk etymology), initial* go-, *also derived from the same words, and roots mentioned above. Also cf* "yo-yo", *zigzag.*]

## GOL

"Loppew gol andáxt." *"She blushed", "Her cheeks became rosy."*
"Kárew gol karde." *"He is doing a brisk business.", "His work is warm or hot."*
"Miyun e dustáw gol karde." *"He is a success among his friends."*
"Ye gol e átew bezár ruy e qelyun e man." *"Put one piece of live charcoal on my water-pipe."*
[*etymology and semantic reconstruction*: gol < garema-, *(Avest)*; घर्म *Ghármá (Sanskrit). also*: gar-m, hor, hor-m, gor-m, xor, xorwid, hur, golxan, gor, gor gereftan, *and most probably Arabic* "hormat" *(this word has all the characteristics of Avestan words, with the suffix*, -mat, = mata,*)*, gole.]

## GOLE GOLE

*This term is applied to anything with spotty distribution.*
"Muháw gole gole rixte." *"He has alopecia areata."*
"Qáli gole gole suxte." *"The rug is burned in a spotty fashion."*
"Gole gole ride o rafte." *"He has excreted feces on various spots on his way."*
[*etymology and semantic reconstruction: I believe,* "gole-gole" *is derived from* "gol" *meaning* "heat, warmth", *see* "gol". *The basic concept being anything similar to small foci of fire, made with bushes and firewood on a field.*]

## GONDE

*Nowadays used synonymous with* "big", *but etymologically it should allude to anything round, rotund, and globose in shape.*
"In otáq godna-s." *"This room is big or large."*
"Ye hendune ye gonde." *"A big watermelon."*
"Ye zan e kun gonde." *"A woman with big fanny."*
[*etymology and semantic reconstruction*: Gonde = gond-e; gondak *(Pahlavi)*, gond *(Armenian) (a ball, sphere) (BQM p.1843).*
*Cf.* qon-ce *(an unopened bud)*; con-d-ak; =gon-d-ak, gond(ak) zadan *(to squat)* qon-d *(to squat)*; gon-bad *(a dome)*; gom-bad *(a dome)*; cán-e *(chin = a round protuberance)*; qom-bol *(a round protuberance)*; con-bátme *(to squat)*; gon-d *(a testis, testicle.).*

38

*Also note the slang term*: gonde-bak *"A term used for depreciation of people with big bodies, as compared with their immature and childish behavior, "gonde-bak" = see "gonde" above. "bak" = bey, bay, beyg, beyk, all derived from "Baq" (Persian) Lord, God. Bhágá (Sanskrit): God, lord.* भगवत *bhágávátá: Pertaining to a God; holy, divine.*]

## GONDE-BAK

*This term is used as a noun, rarely as an adjective. It is applied to adults or older children, who would behave as a child or very immaturely.*
"Gonde-bak árum begir!" *"Be quiet and don't tinker with things, you big child!"*
*etymology: See* "gonde."

## GOR: GORGOR, GOR GEREFTAN, GOR ZADAN

"Gor mizane." *"It is burning with a blazing flame.", "It is blazing."*
"Gor gor misuze." *"It blazes.", "It burns with a blaze."*
"Gor gereft." *"It caught fire."*
"Hey gor migire." *"She is having hot flashes."*
*etymology: See* "gol, *and* "gole-gole".

## GOTREYI = KATREYI

*This is usually used as an adverb:* "Gotreyi mige!" *"He says (something) without a basis."* "Katreyi ye kári mikone" *"He does something, without due thought and consideration or logical evaluation of the circumstances."*
[*etymology: cf* gotre + katre: *cf* katára, katár: *A sort of short sword. cf katárá (Sanskrit).*]

## GUL

"Gul" *is somebody with low IQ* "gul e gul-e!" *"He is such an idiot."*
"Gul zadan." *"To take in, deceive."*
"Gul xordan." *"To be decived."*
"Doxtara ro gul zad o xikkew o bálá ávord." *"He deceived the young girl and filled up her leather bag (made her pregnant.)"*
*etymology: ?: Cf* kur *(blind).*

## GUZ

"Guz" *is the gas passed from the anus, accompanied by a noise.* "Also such noise is called "guz". *In contradistinction to* "guz", "cos" *is a gas passed without noise."*

"guz dádan" *"to pass gas with an audible noise."*

"Guz-beriw dar raft." *A pejorative term:* "*: literally: The guy whose beard be farted, ran away!",*. *"The despicable man ran away."*

*etymology: ?: Probably of onomatopoeic origin.*

# H

## HACAL

"Hacal" *is a noun. It is almost similar to "predicament" i.e. a situation especially one that is dangerous, unpleasant, embarrassing, or sometimes comical.* "Náqolá má ro endáxt tu hacal, xodew jim wod." *"The wicked, shrewd guy, got us involved in a predicament, and disappared on us!"*
[*etymology*: hacal; haca-, *cf* "kawa-," *(Avest)(a cut; gulf)*]

## HAF-HAF; HAF-HAFU

"Haf haf" *is a depreciative term used for the way that very old edentulous people talk.* "Haf haf mikone." *"He speaks like an old edentulous man."* "Boro pir e haf-hafu!" *"Go home! You old, decrepit man, talking in a funny way!"*
[*etymology*: "Haf-haf" *is of onomatopoeic origin. cf with* "háf háf" *= bow-wow, barking sound of a dog.* "Sage háf háf mikone!" *"The dog barks or makes a bow-wow sound."*]

## HALE-HULE

*Used only in reference to poor eating habits. Thus* "Hei hale-hule mixore." *(He eats frequently from various types of foods. He eats all too many different things, very irregularly.)* "Hale-hule naxor!" *(Don't eat junk food!)*
[*etymology*: "hule" *rhyming word with* "hale". hale *&* hule *both: cf* harz, harze, alak, alaki, xol, xole. *All presumably derived from the same root:* harediw (Avest), arak; harak *(Pahlavi):* harz; harze; xers (alaf e xers); harj (harj o marj). *also* "qalat", "xaráb" *(qalat; xaráb? Arabic loanwords, from the same root); also* "xvíle"]

## HARDAMBIL

*This word is used as an adverb.* "Hardambil" *proper is occasionally used alone, as a substantive.*
"Hardambil tokmehá ro fewár dád." *"Not knowing, and in an undisciplined manner, he pushed all the buttons."*
"Hardambili ye cizi goft gereft." *"He uttered something in a totally unprincipled way, and it turned out to be right."*

[*etymology*: hardambil: ? hardam = *every moment and* "bil"? = behel (*from* "hewtan," "helidan," *1- to let; allow. 2- to give up; abandon). cf* bil *(Lori): let, allow. Also cf* "belbewu". *Also cf* bilax, vel, velew, velelew.]

## HARJ O MARJ

*This word means chaos, disturbance, riot.* "Kewvar docár e harj o marj wod." *"The country was in a state of chaos and turmoil."* "Dar harj o marjhá xeylihá kowte wodand." *"Very many people were killed in the riots."*
[*etymology*: Cf* harj, harz & hale hule.
marj: Cf* á + marj (Sanskrit): to wipe off. Also cf. ámorzidan, to forgive ámareaen (Avest)(They forgive), from the same Sanskrit root. "to wipe off." (Grundriss der iranischen Philologie - Geiger and Kuhn, vol. 1, part 2, p.56.), also cf. marnjenitan (Pahlavi) (BF p.363): to destroy, to ruin, to kill.*]

## HATAK-O-PATAK

*Used only as* "Hatak o patak e kasi rá páre kardan". *Knock someone out. To punish someone (usually bodily) so that the opponent is totally disabled and ruined.*
[*etymology*: hatak, patak. *Change the first vowels to* "á"---"hátak", *and* "pátak", *meaning* "defense" *and* "anti-attack" *respectively.*
"Há-," *is a common prefix especially in Iranian dialects, substituted in modern Persian mostly by* "be-," *in forming the imperative mood. Thus* "hágir" (Begir!) (Take!); "Háde!" (Bede!)(Give!); cf* "Hácin o vácin!" "Ye pát o vácin!"
Tak *derived from* "takidan" *(to run; to attack)*
*Thus* "hatak" *(attack) and* "patak" *(anti-attack) (defense). Thus* "hatak o patak e kasi rá páre kardan" *(To break/ smash someone's means of attack and defense, thus rendering him defenseless and disabled.)*]

## HAVU

*In societies where polygamy is practiced (by men),* "havu" *is the word for each new wife, in relation to the previous wife or wives. Sometimes* "havu" *is used to refer to these wives, without considering the priority. Also any person who is newcomer and impinges on the rights of his or her predecessors is called a* "havu".
"Havu ye ham-an." *"They are rival wives." "They both share one husband."*

"Mage havu ye man-i?" *"Are you my "havu"? (rival)? (You are impinging on my rights and your position is unjust.)*
[etymology: *cf* hunu *(Avest) (son, daughter, for demoniacal creatures)* <hu *(Avest)(to deliver or give birth for demoniacal creatures)* (Purdávud, Yasht-ha, I, p.234); *also cf* "an" *(soft, unformed stool) (fig. a worthless despicable creature; used for the child born by a "havu" rival wife.)*]

## HÁJ O VÁJ

*Almost always used as a noun, meaning with gaping eyes, and mouth due to extreme surprise.* "Háj o váj mundam". *"I was dumbfounded."* "Háj o váj istád o berr o berr negá kard." *"He stood there with gaping eyes and mouth and watched."*
*etymology:?*

## HÁRT O PURT

*This term is used when referring to giving orders and commands, in a haughty manner. The term is depreciative and means that the person giving orders or commands does not have much authority and wants to impress people by making noise, and bombastic remarks.* "Kamtar hárt o purt kon!" *"Stop your ordering people around, nobody listens to you!"*
*etymology*: "Hárt" *is most probably of onomatopoeic origin.* "Purt" *is a coword, commonly used in Persian, such as* "áwqál páwqál", "qáti páti", "henzer penzer."]

## HENZER PENZER

*This term denotes objects, usually old and of no value, junk.*
"Ye mowt henzer penzer ávord be má qáleb kone." *"He brought some worthless things and wanted to talk us into buying them!"*
[*etymology*: "Penzer" *is a coword for* "henzer". *See* "hárt o purt".
"henzer" ≡ "panjar":
"Jálán जालं" *(Sanskrit): metal lattice work. A coat of mail.*
*Cf* "calan", "calangar", *also* "calan" = "zereh" = "jouwan". *All of the same root.*
panjara = panj-jara = panj + jálán: *five pieces of metallic, lattice-work make a cage, thus* panjar = panzer. *metallic objects, such as a cage, or lattice-work.*]

## HER-HER; HERR-HERR

*Her her is a term used for laughing loud.*
"Herr herr nakon!" "Herr herr nazan!" = *"don't laugh loud!"*
"Doxtare ye herr-herru!" *"A joking term: "Hey , you laughing girl! –you who laughs loud and makes too much noise." "You –loud- laughing girl!"*
[*etymology*: *"herr herr" is an onomatopoeic word.*]

## HERRI!

"Herri!" *is a term used usually in imperative sense, meaning "Get out of here!" "Leave here!". It is pejorative and is usually used alone. Thus:* "Nemixáhi kár koni? Pas herri!". *("Don't you want to work? Then get out of here!")*
[*etymology*: *cf* herru *(far)(Armenian),* herránál *(to go away)(Armenian)* herráxos *(telephone).*]

## HEY

"Hey *is a verbal particle, meaning a repetition of an action."*
"Hey bezan!" *"Beat and beat!"*
"Hey boxor!" *"Eat and eat!"*
"Hey bordim, báz umad." *"We took or carried it away repeatedly, but it continued coming back."*
[*etymology*: hey = hami = mi, *Also cf* "de-" *(verbal particle)* = hamiwe *(always)*
*compare*: hey raftam = hami-raftam = mi-raftam *cf* "de-raftam", "de-boro".]

## HIR O VIR

"Hir o vir" *denotes a state of full activity and being extremely busy.*
"Tu ye in hir-o-vir umade az man ci miporse!" *"See, he is asking me such a silly question, in the full swing of business!"*
"Miyun e hir o vir, biyá zir abrum o begir!" *(proverb): In the middle of brisk business, she asks me to pluck her eyebrows (A silly request).*
[*etymology: ?*hir o vir: *cf* juwidan hervir *(Spanish)(to boil)*
yaiw-, *(Avest); yiw (Sanskrit) yuw-, (Sanskrit)(to boil; simmer seethe.)*]

## HIZ

*I disregard the classical meanings given for this word, not in common use now.*
"Hiz" *is usually referred to a man, who is sex-obsessed and looks at women*

44

with lustful eyes or makes improper approaches. "Hiz" is usually used as a substantive. "Xeyli hiz-e!" "He is very hiz". "Hizi az cewmew mibáre." "His looks are lustful."
etymology: ?

## HOL

"hol dádan" "to push, to shove": "Miz o ye kam hol bede in var." "Push the table a little this way."
"hol zadan": to rush, act hurriedly. "Cerá hol mizani?" "Why you rush?"
etymology: ?

## HOLOFDUNI, HOLOFTUNI

"Bábá ro gereftan o kardan tu holofduni." "He was arrested and sent to jail."
"Holofduni" is usually used synonymous with "jail", however with the connotation of imprisonment without trial and usually without any hope of salvage. Thus one may disappear without any trace, after being put in a "Holofduni."
[etymology: ? <√ homb.
holofduni = holoftuni = holof-dun-i,: tun-i, = dun-i-, = dáni.: -dán = a place, a vessel, a receptacle. e.g.: gol-dán = a flower vase; namakdán = salt-cellar.
holoft = hoft = homb, honb: cf. "ne-hof-t-an": to hide. = "ne-homb-id-an."
also cf.: "nehoftan", nehonbidan", "xomb", "xonb", "xomre", xonbre", "nehanban".]

## HOQQE

"hoqqe", a humbug.
"hoqqe zadan" to play a trick on someone.
"hoqqe xordan" to be taken in.
"Xub hoqqeyi behew zadiyá!" "You played a good trick on him!" "You fooled him very nicely."
etymology: ?

## HORM

"Tu horm e tanur váynassá." "Don't stand near the baking oven, where the heat wave (may bother you)."
"Horm e átiw tu ye sarmá xeyli keyf dáwt." "The heat (wave) of the blazing fire was very pleasant in the cold (weather)."

45

[*etymology: See* "gol", "gole-gole".]

## HORT

"hort kewidan": *to suck noisily.* "Hort bekew!" *"Suck it up!"*
"Hort hort hamaw o xord." *"He swallowed the entire thing with lots of noise."*
*etymology: See* "qort".

## HOU

1- "hou kardan" = *to boo*
"Tá umad soxanráni kone houw kardan." *"As soon as he started to speak they booed him."*
"Hou, hou!" *"Boo to you!"*
2- *Used only as* "yek hou". "Yek hou dád zad". *"He cried all of a sudden."*
"Yek hou boxor." *"Drink all of it, in one single breath."*
[*etymology*: "hou" #1, is most probably of onomatopoeic origin.
"hou" #2: ? hou = havá]

## HOUCI

"Houci" *is a heckler, or bawler. Somebody who tries to have things his own way by false propaganda, making lots of noise in order to attract attention.*
"Mixád bá houcigari dádgáh o gul bezane." *"He wants to win the case (in the court) by deceiving the jury, by false and loud propaganda."*
"Martike ye houci, áberu nadáre.!" *"The dishonest man, is a heckler."*
*etymology*: houci = hou-ci: *see* hou #1.

## HOUL

"houl wodan": *to be frightened and thus to lose one's control and not to be able to act rationally.*
"Houl wod o natunest be ámuzegár pásox bede." *"He was frightened, and he lost control and thus he could not answer the teacher properly."*
"Houl nawou!" *"Take your time!"* *"Don't lose your head!"*
"houl kardan" *(vt, and vi)* 1- *(vi): to be shocked, to be extremely frightened.*
"Doxtare houl kard o baccaw o endáxt." *"The young woman was shocked and she had a miscarriage."* 2- *(vt): to make someone hurry.* "Man o houl kardi, kár xaráb wod." *"You made me hurry, thus the mess."*
*etymology:* "houl" < "haul" *(Arabic): to awe, to strike someone with fear, to terrify, to alarm, to frighten.*

46

# I

## IKBIR, IKBIRI

"Ikbir", *and* "ikbiri" *and both used interchangeably, as a substantive.*
"Ikbir(i)" *means, extremely ugly; disgustingly ugly.* "Doxtare ye ikbiri, hey qer
miyád!" *"The disgustingly ugly girl, makes danceful or coquettish
movements."* "Ikbir(i) biyá!" *"Come on, you ugly one!"*
[*etymology: ? cf* aka *(Avest)* + bara

## IWI

*This term is used only as* "iwi iwi" *and commonly followed by* "qorbunet
beram."
*Thus* "iwi-iwi, qorbunet beram."
*meaning: This is an endearing idiom. It means " (my) love,(my) love, may I die
for you."*
*The idiom is used primarily addressing the newborns or babies, who are lovely
and may do interesting things.*
[*etymology :* "iwi" *most probably derived from* "aew" *(Avest)(to wish; to
desire);*
*The Arabic word* "ewq" *is a loanword, with the suffix* "-ka"
*All derived from the root* "iw"," iww" *(Avestan) (to wish, to desire)*
*With* "-ka" *suffix:* iw+ka: iska (Soqlábi) = is-ka *(love; passion)*
"iw" *(Sanskrit)(to wish)*
*Ref: Mohammad Moqadam.* Irán Kude #12, "Sorud e Bonyád e Din e Zartowt",
*Faravahar Publishing Co. 1363, pp 46, 47.*]

# J

### JAFANG

"Jafang" *is a substantive. It means "idle talk", a "nonsensical comment".*
"Jafang nagu!" *"Don't say nonsense!"*
"Jafang-e!" *"It's nonsense!"*
[*etymology: ?: cf* źutan *(Pahlavi):* "źu-t-an", "źuy-", *1- to swallow or eat, for devilish creatures. 2- to talk much 3- to stammer. (BF Pp.675,676)*]

### JALQ

"Jalq" *means "masturbation".* "Jalq zadan" *means "to masturbate".*
"jalq dar zir e dalq xow báwad." (Obeyd e Zákán) *"Masturbation is most enjoyable under a cloak."* (Obeyd e Zákán).
*etymology:? cf* "jalq": "zalq" *(Arabic)*

### JAMBAL

*See* "jádu jambal".

### JAQUR PAQUR

*This is the term for a Persian dish made from minced liver, roasted with onion and eggs.* "Jaqur-paqur xord o ráh oftád." *"He ate some* "Jaqur-paqur" *and set out."*
[*etymology:* "paqur" *is a coword for* "jaqur" *eg.* "pul-mul"; "jaqur" = "jegar" *(liver)*.]

### JÁDU JAMBAL

"Jádu-jambal" *means "sorcery", or "all sorts of procedures and techniques used in witchcraft."*
"Rafte jádu-jambal karde, wouharew o ciz-xor karde, ke kalak e havuw o bakkane." *"She has resorted to witchcraft and has made her husband drink a voodoo medicine in order to get rid of the incumbent or new wife of her husband."*
[*etymology:* jádu < yátu-, *(Avest) (magician),* yátu *(Old Ind.),* játuk *(Pahlavi) (BQM, 553) cf* योगः yogáh *(Sanskrit): (a charm, spell, magic, magical art).*
"jambal" √?]

## JEQEL

*This word is used as a substantive. It is referred to an individual (usually a child or adolescent), who is short for his age and is very astute, or shrewd, considering his size or age. a rogue, a cheat.*
"Jeqel, biyá injá!" *"Come here you shrewd midget!"*
"Pesare ye jeqele man o gul zad." *"The shrewd or clever midget, took me in."*
[*etymology: Cf* jeqel, woqál: *cf.* शृगाल *wrigálá (Sanskrit): 1-a jackal 2- A cheat, rogue, swindler. Also cf* "tagel" *(young)*]

## JER

1- "Jer zadan" means *"to go back on one's word". "Also in games it means "not to accept the rules of the game". "*Tu bázi hey jer mizane." *"He constantly breaks the rules of the game."*
"Goft, agar man bordam, sad toman mide, ammá jer zad o nadád." *"He said that he would give me 100 Tomans, if I win, but he went back on his word, and did not give anything."*
2- "jer" = tear, "jer xordan", *"to be torn apart".* "jer dádan" *"to tear apart".* "Piranew gereft be tiq o jer xord." *"His shirt got caught on the spikes and was torn apart."*
*etymology: ?*

## JEZQÁLE

"Jezqále" *is a substantive. Anything deeply burned, and shrunken is called* "jezqále". *sizzled and fried.*
"Tadig suxt o jezqále wod." *"The cooked rice at the bottom of the pot burned to charcoal."*
[*etymology*: jezqále: jez-qál-e: jez = suz, suxtan. *See* "jezz o vezz".
-qál, qále *(suffix) eg*: "dás-qále", *a small sickle*
"boz-qále", *a small goat, a kid;* "kan-qále": *a girl; young female slave*]

## JEZ(Z) O VEZ(Z), JELEZ(Z) O VELEZ(Z)

"Jezz o vezzew darumad." *"It started burning making a crackling sound.", "It started sizzling."*
"Eláhi ke jezz e jegar bezani!" *"May God inflict a bad punishment on you, so you will mourn bitterly (so your liver may burn)" "So your liver may sizzle".*
"Jezz" *is used to denote anything burning specially with a sizzling noise.*

[*etymology*: jez = jelez, suz, suztan, *to burn*.

vez = velez, beriz, berewtan, beryán.

*Cf* suz,; suztan, jez *sizzle*, jezqále.

vez, velez, viliz, beriz, berizan, berijan, beryán, berewtan.]

## JIK

jik zadan; jik-jik kardan; jk-o-vik

"Jik" *is usually used in combinations noted above.*

"Jik zadan", *usually used in negative form.*

*example*: "Jik nazad.", "Jikew darnayumad." *(He/She did not utter a word. He/She did not say anything.)*

"jik-jik kardan" *(of birds: to chirp, to twitter)*

*example*: "Gonjiwke jik-jik mikone."*(The sparrow is chirping.)*

"jik-o-vik" *(friendly or secret talk)*

*example*: "Un do doxtar ba' ham jik-o-vik da'ran." *(Those two girls are very intimate and they have secret talks with each other.)*

[*etymology*: "jik" *could be converted to* "vik", *with* "j", *changing to* "z", "z'" *and* "v".

*Thus the word* "jik" *is of the same root as* "voice" *in English,* "voix" *in French* "vox" *in Latin, and* "váźe","váj" *in Persian.*

*The root is* "vac" *(medic)(to cry); and* "vác-," *(Sanskrit)(to speak) and* "vac" *(Avest)(to speak).*

## JIM

"Jim wodan" *"to disappear", "to leave surreptitiously."* "Tá did havá pase jim wod." *"As soon as he realized that the circumstances were unfavorable, he disappeared."*

[*etymology*: √ ?: 1- jim *cf* "gom" *(to be lost)(lost)*

         2- jim *cf* "jam" *(The ancient Persian king, who had a cap, which, once when worn, made him invisible.)*]

## JIQ

jiq: *scream; screaming*

"jiq zadan", "jiq kewidan": *(to scream).*

*example*: "Cera' jiq mizani?" *(Why do you scream?)*

"jiq-o-viq" *(talk loudly and irrationally; talk loudly and insultingly)*

[*etymology:* "j" *in* "jiq" *could convert to* "z"," z'" *and* "v". *Thus* jiq o viq.

[*etymology: See the explanation under "jik".*]

## JIR

*This term is usually used as* "jir-jir kardan". *(to creak)*
*example:* "In taxtexa'b jir-jir mikone." *(This bed (frame) creaks.)*
"Suske jir jir mikone." *(The cockroach is chirring.)*
*etymology: See the explanation under* "jik", *and compare* "jir" *with* "jiq".

## JIW = wáw

*This word is used for* "urine" *when talking to infants, and children. Thus*
"jiw", *means* "urine"; "jiw kardan" = *to urinate, to pee*
"Nini, cerá tu ját jiw kardi?" "*You little baby, why did you wet your bed?*"
[*etymology:* mixtan *(to urinate),* mize *(urine):* meha मेह *(Sanskrit)(urine):*
m→b→v→j; h→s→w] wáw

## JOANLAQ

*This is a pejorative word commonly applied to a man, who is considered to be*
*of low social rank, and not knowledgeable, aspiring high goals or ideals, or*
*interfering with something beyond his capability.*
"Martike ye joanlaq umade be man dastur e hesábdári mide." "*(Look at) the*
*despicable man, who is teaching me how to keep the accounts!*"
*etymology:* joalnaq = joal-naq. joal *(Arabic): beetle, dung-beetle.;* -naq, = nák
*(suffix), making adjective (usually depreciative or unpleasant) from nouns.*

## JOFTAK

"Joftak" *is a kick by both hind-legs of a quadruped, usually donkeys, mules, or*
*similar beasts of burden. When applied to men it is pejorative and it is used*
*with* "zadan", *or* "endáxtan", *signifying unwise rejection of a favorable offer or*
*opportunity.*
"Harce pesare názew o mikewe, doxtar e xol joftak mindáze." "*The more the*
*young man, is kind to her, she behaves in a stupid manner rejecting him.*"
"Xare joftak zad toxmew o qor kard." "*The donkey kicked his testes, due to*
*which he developed hydrocele.*"
[*etymology:* joftak = joft-ak; -ak, *suffix.*: Joft = jof-t: युगः yugáh *(Sanskrit) a*
*yoke.* युज् yuj *(Sanskrit): to join, unite, attach. Thus:* "joftak": *two legs joined*
*together, directly from the root described above. Also see:* "jukki"]

## JOL

*This word is applied to a place of cloth usually old, tattered or worn out.*
"Ásemun jol-e." *"He is a pauper."* *"His cover is the sky."* "Jol o palásew o vardáwt o raft." *"He picked up his clothes and rags, and went away."*
"Boro jol o paláset o jamm kon!" *"Go away from this place! Pick up your rags."*
[*etymology*: "jol", *also see* "jolombor":
*Cf* जीर्ण *jirná (Sanskrit)(1- old, ancient 2- worn out, ruined, wasted, tattered (as cloth)]*
जराण *járáná (Sanskrit)(1- old 2- decayed 3- infirm)*
जरा *jará (1-old age 2- decrepitude, infirmity)*]

## JOLOMBOR

"Jolombor" *is somebody in a garment in rags. Somebody wearing any outfit which is old and tattered.*
"Martike ye jolombor." *"The man in rags" (depreciative term)*
"Ye zan e jolombor oftáde donbálew." *"A woman in rags followed him."*
[*etymology*: jolombor: jol-ombor: jol, *see* "jol"
ombor? ambar = an-bar = andar-bar, *One wearing....*
"jolombor": *One wearing a* "jol", *a tattered garment.*]

## JUKKI

*This word originally used to mean "an Indian practicing yoga", now means somebody awfully lean, skinny, and ugly.* "Mardike ye jukki, be rixt e xodew nigá nemikone, donbál e doxtar e man miyofte." *"Look at the ugly man, a bag of bones, who does not look at himself (in a mirror), but he chases my daughter."*
[*etymology*: Jukki *from* युगः *yugáh (Sanskrit), a yoke;* युज् yuj युक्त yukta: *to join, unite, attach, to yoke, harness.* "jukki" = *a yogi, one whose "self" is united with the "eternal self".*]

52

# K

## KABLÁYI

*Also see "Mawdi".*

*"Kabláyi" is a way of addressing both men and women. It apparently originates from the name of the Holy city of "Karbalá", where several Moslem leaders are buried. A man or woman who has made a pilgrimage to "Karbalá" is thus called "Kabláyi" thus:* "Kabláyi Mammad az deh umad." *"Mr. Mohammad came from the village."*

## KAL

*"Kal" means: 1- bald, 2- somebody whose hair is lost, due to ringworm, etc.* "Kal agar tabib budi, sar e xod davá namudi." *"(Sa-,di)" If the bald man were truly a physician, he should have had cured his baldness first."*
[*etymology*: kal, = kacal.
*cf* खलती khalati *(bald, bald-headed)*
*kalák (Sanskrit): a treeless plain, steppe.*]

## KALAK

*"Kalak" has two different meanings.*
1- kalak = *a trick.* "kalak zadan" *"to play a trick on...."* "Be dustew kalak zad." *"He played a trick on his friend."* "kalak xordan" *"To be taken in"* "Yáru bad kalaki xord." *"The so-and-so person, was badly deceived."*
2- *Always with* "kandan": "Kalak e cizi yá kasi rá kandan": *"To finish up with something, to eat or use up."* "Kalak e kasi rá kandan": *"To get rid of someone. To kill, eliminate or do away with someone."* "Kalak e wirini ro kand." *"He ate up all the cake."* "Kalak e dowman o kand." *"He eliminated the foe."*
[*etymology*: kalak: #1 *cf* कलहः *kaláháh (Sanskrit);* कलहं *kalahan (Sanskrit): (a trick, deceit, falsehood.)*
kalak #2 *(See above)? cf with* kalle = kal-le, *head.?* kal = *head.*]

## KALÁFE

*This term is mostly used as an adjective.* "Kaláfe wodan" *"to be frustrated."*

53

"kaláfe wodam." *"I became frustrated."* "kaláfe" *signifies an emotional state in which an individual loses self-control and is given to despair, restlessness and anxiety.* "Vaqti didamew pák kaláfe bud." *"When I saw her, she was in utter anxiety and despair, or distress."*
[*etymology*: kaláfe = kaláf-e; *cf* "kaláf" *a skein of yarn.* kaláf = kaláve, = kalábe: "Sar e kaláf o gom karde." *"He has lost the head (lead) of the yarn in a skein."* ie *"He is confused and misled."* Thus "kaláfe" *similar to a* "kaláf" *confused, with no way out.*
*etymology*, √ ?]

## KALFATÁR, KALFATTÁR

*This is a substantive, commonly used in vocative case. Thus:* "Ey kalfattár!" "kalfattár" *is used to refer to an individual who is of rude manners. He is quarrelsome and may attack with minimal stimulation.*
[*etymology and semantic reconstruction*: kal-fat(t)-ár
kal-, *cf* xar-, *in* "xarpul" *(multimillionaire)*, xar-zur *(very strong)*, xar-guw *(rabbit, the one with big ears)*, xar-, *and its equivalents* kal-, qara-, qol-, *and* gul-, *all mean big, megalo-, coarse. Other examples with this prefix:* qara-caman *(big pasture)*; qara-márs *(defeated very badly in backgammon game) (This* qara-, *is not related with the Turkish word* "qara *(black))*; kir *(penis)*; kal *(mountain goat)*; qolve *(kidney)*; qolve-sang *(big rock)*; qul-tawan *(gigantic; corpulent)*
-ár: *This is a suffix forming either adjectives or nouns, eg:* "xarid-ár" *(buyer; purchaser)*; "goft-ár *(speech; discussion)*; did-ár *(visiting). In* kal-fat(t)-ár, "ár" *is the suffix denoting doer of an action like* "xaridár" *and* "ámuxtár". "fat" *derived from the same root as* "fetádan" *and* "oftádan". √ *pát (Sanskrit) (to fall down, come down, set, cast oneself at, etc).*
*Thus* kal-fatt-ár = *a big attacker. Other words of this root, i.e.* √ pát: pátál *(very old and prone to fall)*; áfat; vafát; fout *(Arabic loan-words.)*]

## KALLÁW

*A sponger, swindler, parasite.*
*This word is used as a substantive.* "Barádarew kalláw e bozorgi-ye." *"His brother is a big swindler."* "Bá kalláwi xune o máwin xarid." *"He has bought a house and a car, by swindling."*
*etymology*: kalláw = qalláw < Turkish: "qalláw" (FM)
[*root: ?*]

54

## KALPATRÁYI

*This is an adjective or adverb.  It means "in an inconsiderate fashion", "to deal with a problem without proper understanding"*
*examples:* "Kalpatráyi mige!" *(He says that without proper thinking and consideration.)* "Nemitunam kalpatráyi bimár rá darmán konam." *(I cannot treat the patient in a hit or miss fashion.)*
*etymology:* kal-pat-trá-yi
kal-, *see* "gerán" *(big, heavy, coarse, etc)* "qolcomáq", "qoldor"
pat-, *see* "oftádan" <√ *pat (Sanskrit) (to fall; to cast oneself at, etc)*
-trá, *cf* तृ *tri (Sanskrit)(sign of participle; doer of...)*
*Thus* "kal-patra-", *"a big attacker; One who casts oneself on something/somebody, coarsely and in an inconsiderate manner."*

## KAMEW

*Used only as* "Kur-am, kamew-am." *This term is used in describing somebody's indiscriminate manners in eliminating everybody in the way of reaching one's goal.  One killing everybody blindly.  Literally: "I am blind and I am "kamesh"* "Cerá kur-am kamew-am darávordi?" *"Why did you fire everybody indiscriminately?"*
[*etymology:* kamew = kam-ew, *most probably* = gáv-miw, *a buffalo.  Thus a symbol of brute force, and unguided violence.*]

## KAP, KAPIDAN

*This word is usually used in the following fashion:*
"Bekap!" *"Sit down and keep quiet!"  An imperative form from* "kapidan."
"Kape ye margew o gozowt." *"He finally either died, or slept, and became quiet."*
"Kape ye marget o bezár!" *"Lie down and die, or keep quiet!"*
[*etymology:* "xapak", "xafak", *(Pahlavi)* = suffocated, hanged.  Also cf "xaf", "xafa", "xaba", *(choking, dyspnea),* "xabide" *(choked, suffocated),* "xapa", *and* "xapak".]

## KAPAL

"Kapal", *or* "kafal", *means the protuberance of the gluteal muscles, on the two sides of the anus, and intergluteal fissure.*
"Nigá! Doxtare kun o kapalew o endáxte birun o qer mide." *"Look! That girl has bared her fanny and is making danceful movements."*

[*etymology*: √?: kap. *cf* kuh, kuf, → kup, kap, qonb-ol. kapal = kap-al, -al, -ul, -ol: *a suffix, cf* "baqal" *(axilla, bossom), cf* "kew-ále", *(groin)* –al, = ál, *cf* "domb-ál".]

## KAT

"Kat" *means "the upper arms" and it is used only in the following combinations.* "Az kat oftádam." *"My upper arms are falling., ie I am awfully tired. (physically exerted myself, in some work needing muscular power)."*
*Also* "az kat o kul oftan" *(to have very tired arms and back.)*
"Kat baste bordanew zendun." *"He was carried to the jail, with arms tied (to the chest)."*
*etymology*: "kat", *cf* "kaft", "koft", "ketf", *all meaning "shoulder".*

## KAT O KOLOFT

"Páyehá ye in miz xeyli kat o koloft-e." *"The legs of this table are very coarse and thick."*
"Can tá kat o koloft behew endáxt." *"He told him a few rude words."*
*In contrast to other Iranian dialects,* "kat" *is not used by itself, in* "Tehráni" *slang. It is commonly used in combination with* "koloft" = *thick.* "kat" = "gat" *means anything big, cumbersome and usually unshapely.*
[*etymology*: kat (Mázandaráni *dialect*) = *big.*
*Cf* गाढ *gádh* (Sanskrit) *1- thick, dense, 2- strong, vehement.*]

## KATREYI

*See* "gotreyi".

## KAWKUL

"Kawkul" *is a wooden or metallic container suspended by a chain carried by a dervish. The chain of the* "kawkul" *is placed on the shoulder, and the container is placed by the side of the body or along the anterior axillary lines.*
[*etymology: The following etymology derivation is from FM (Dr. M. Moyin):*
kawkul = kaw-kul, = kaj-kul. kul = *back, the upper part of one's back,* "Kaj" *not straight, slanting, tilted.*
*I believe* "kawkul" *is made of* "kaw", *and* "kul". "kul" *is derived from* कुलाय *kuláyáh, or* कुलायं *kuláyán (Sankrit), which means "a case or receptacle".*
*Thus* "kawkul" *is a case or receptacle carried on one's* "kaw" "kaw" = *armpit,*

56

*armhole* = कुझझः *kakwáhwáh.. Another version would be* "kaw" *from* कशः: *kawáh, or* कशा *kawá, (Sanskrit) a string, a rope. Thus* "kawkul", *is a vessel carried by a string or a rope (hanging the vessel.)*]

# KÁKÁ

"Káká" *means* "a brother". "Hesáb hesáb, káká barádar." *"Reckoning is reckoning, and* "káká", *is a* "brother". *"Don't show any partisanship, and deal in a just manner." "Don't expect any favors, and expect a fair deal."* "kákásiyá." *"A negro."*
"Káko sey kon!" *(Shirazi dialect)* *"Look brother!"*
[*etymology*: káká = brother. "káku = *maternal uncle, mother's brother.* kákuye *(Mazandarani dialect)* = *maternal uncle.*
káko (Shirazi) = *brother.* √?]

# KÁKOL

*This word is applied to a bunch of hair usually at the top of the head. Also the ear of a corn is called* "kákol". *The crest of birds, is also called* "kákol".
"Ye pesar e kakol zari baráw záyid." *"She bore (gave birth to) a boy with blond forelock, for him (her husband.)"*
"Ye morq e kákoli" *"A crested hen or bird."*
[*etymology: Cf* kákol = *crest, forelock;* kolála = *forelock.:* koláh = *a hat*; kalál = *vertex of the head, from forehead to the top of the head.*
*The basic concept is:* "a sign of good birth".
*All derived from or related to*: कुलिक *kulika* = कुलक *kulaka (Sanskrit) of good family, of good birth.* कुलतः: *kulátáh (by birth);* कुल्य *kulya* = *well-born, related to a family or race;* कुल्यः: *kulyáh a respectable man.*]

# KÁL

"Kál" *means* "green, unripe".
"Sib e kál naxor del dard migiri." *"Don't eat unripe apples, you'll get belly ache."*
[*etymology:* "kál", *cf* कल *kala (adjective) crude, undigested.*]

# KEKE

"Keke varcin."

"Keke" *meaning "feces" is almost exclusively used as* "keke varcin" *in Tehrani slang.* "Keke" *is primarily a word for "feces" in the Ispahani dialect.* "Keke varcin" *is somebody who is very stingy, one who collects even feces in order to make money out of it.*

"Keke varcin, puli beham zade, xiyál mikone ádam wode." *"The man who was a feces-collector, is now rich, and he thinks that he has become important."*

*etymology:* √?: *Cf* "goh".

## KELENJÁR

*This word is almost always used with* "raftan". *Thus* "kelenjár raftan" *means "to fight with someone", "to struggle with....", "to haggle"*

"Cerá bá man kelenjár miri?" *"Why do you fight with me?" "Why you argue with me?"*

"Hame ye wab bá in máwin kelenjár raft." *"He was struggling all night long, with this car (in order to fix it)."*

[*etymology*: kelenjár = kárezár: *battle, fight,* < kár, -zár. *Directly derived from*: kárejár *(Pahlavi)*: kár = *fight*, kára-, *(Old Persian)* = *army*; káras *(litauisch) battle, (BQM p.1560).*

## KENEF

"Kenef" *or* "keneft" *is usually used with* "kardan" *or* "wodan". "Kenef kardan" = *to disgrace someone.* "kenef wodan": *to be disgraced.*

"Mádarew jelo ye dustáw mocew o váz kard, bicáre xeyli kenef wod." *"His mother exposed (his lie), in front of his friend, he was badly disgraced."*

*etymology:* √?

## KENES

*This word is used as a substantive. It means somebody who loves money, and does not like to spend money even for himself or even for necessary causes.*

"Pedarew kenes o cos xor-e, be cube azgil mimune, nemiwe tiqew zad." *"His father is very stingy, and he does not spend money on anything (= cos-xor), he is like the wood of hazelnut tree (very hard), you can not get juice out of it by cutting it with a razor."*

*etymology:* √?

## KEREWME

*Commonly used in combination with* "náz", "kerewme" *means,* "*making sweet gestures, and attractive movements, especially by the eyes, and lips.*"

"Náz kardan", *means that somebody, especially a girl or woman, who likes to do something, or to eat something, or to make love with a boy, pretends that she does not like it, however her mien, and behavior show that she really likes it.*

"Ce náz o kerewmeyi! Ki mire in hame ráh o." *"She is very coquettish."*
[*etymology: cf* "qerewmál"
*cf* "karaw", "karas", "karawidan", "karasidan": *to deceive by fawning and flattery.*
√?: *Cf* कर्ष: *kárwáh = kársáh: (Sanskrit): 1- drawing, pulling 2- attracting.*
कर्षक *karwáká (Sanskrit): One who, or what draws, attracts, cf with* "kewidan" = *to pull, to attract.*]

## KERR O FERR

"Kerr o ferr" *is almost synonymous with* "*pomp and circumstances.*"
"Bá hame ye kerr o ferrew sar e xarj e arusi ye doxtarew vámunde." *"Despite all his pomp, he is not able to defray the expenses of his daughter's marriage ceremony."*
[*etymology:* √? *cf* kerrenidan *(Pahlavi)(to create for daevic creatures.) MK p.109*]

## KEWIDE

*A slap on the face.*
"Kewide zad behew, mallaq wod." *"He gave him a slap on the face, and he was knocked out."* "Kewide xord ádam wod." *"He received a slap on the face, and since then he is behaving."*
[*etymology:* kewide = kew-id-e: *I doubt that* "kewide" *meaning* "a slap on the face" *is derived from* "kewidan" = *to pull:* √ karw-, *(Avest),* karw-, *(Sanskrit) to pull. (BQM p.1657): cf* कश: kawáh, *and* कशा kawá *(Sanskrit): 1- A whip, 2- flogging.*]

## KEZ

1- "Kez kardan" *to squat, to sit in a squatting or stooping fashion, usually in grief, or from cold.*

"Havá sard bud o hame ye jujehá kez karde budan." *"It was cold and all chickens were squatting."*

2- "kez xordan" = *to shrink and become curled up, such as wool singed by fire.*
"Sibilew kez xord." *"His mustache (was exposed to fire, and it) was singed."*

3- "kez dádan": "Korkew o kez bede." *"Singe its nap." "Burn it superficially so its nap is singed."*

[*etymology:* "kez", *semantically of the same primary concept, as:* quz, guź, kuź, kuze, quze, gouz, *etc. Also cf* कुब्ज kubj: *(Sanskrit): hump-backed.*]

## KIR

*penis, an erect penis.*

"Hálá vase ye má kir waqqi mikoni?" *"Now you've become stubborn and you want to give me (us) hard time?"* (Literally: *Now you are (showing) us an erect penis?"*

"Kir e xar o kos e áhu!" *"Donkey's penis and deer's vulva!"* (A comparison to show extreme incompatibility between two things, one being delicate and small, the other coarse, rough and big.)

[*etymology:* See "dul"; cor *(penis);* "cul" *in* cácul *and* kal *in* "kafatár"]

## KIS

*This word means 1- a wrinkle, a crease, 2- crumpled, specifically on a piece of cloth or on clothing.*

"Walváram kis wod." *"My pants are creased (wrinkled)".*

"Injáw kis xorde, kisew o báz kon (otu kon)." *"Here (the garment) is wrinkled, or creased, you must remove the crease (you must press it out)."*

[*etymology:* "kis". *Cf* "kaj", "kaź", *crooked, slanting, tilted. See:* "kez."]

## KIW

"kiw-kiw": *This is used to incite a dog to attack.*

"kiw dádan": *to incite a dog to attack.*

"kiw kardan": *to chase the birds away.*

"Pesare umad birun saga ro kiw dád o goft "kiw-kiw!" ammá sagá az já najonbidan." *"The young boy came out and incited the dogs, to attack and said "kish-kish", but the dogs did not budge."*

"Morqá dáwtan mivehá ro mixordan, kiwewun kardam." *"The birds were eating (pecking at) the fruits, I shooed them away."*

"Magsá ro kiw kon!"  *"Shoo the flies away!"*
*etymology:* √?

# KOL

"Kol" *is used mostly as an adjective.  It means anything cut or snipped short,
with a stump-shaped remnant, thus:*
"Morq e dom-kol."  *"A hen with a stumpy tail, whose tail is cut too short."*
"Cerá mut o kol kardi?"  *"Why did you cut your hair (too) short?"*
[*etymology and semantic reconstruction*: cf. kol, kudak, kutáh, kucak.  kautaka
*(Avest)* = kucak = *small;* kut *(Old Persian),* "kauta-, kautaka *(Avest).  Also cf*
"kote" *(a child, an offspring-pejorative, also a litter)*]

# KOLOFT

*This word is commonly used as an adjective and occasionally as a noun.*
"Labew xeyli koloft-e."  *"Her lips are very thick."*
[*etymology:* √? *cf* dul.
*Also cf* koloft, kol, dul, kir, *and* स्थूल sthul *(Sanskrit)* = *thick*]

# KOLUCE

*This is a sort of cake made of two crusts and stuffed with jam or preserve.*
"Koluce ye Mázandarán xeyli xowmaza-s."  *"Mazandaran pies are very good-
tasting."*
[*etymology*: koluce = kol-uc-e; cf "kol". xordan; xor → kol + –uce *(suffix)* = -c,
-ic, ice, ize, iźe]

# KOLUX

"Kolux-andáz rá pádáw sang ast."  *"The one who attacks by throwing a mud-
brick, must be punished by a rock."*
[*etymology*: kaluk *(Pahlavi): broken brick, mud-brick*]

# KOMÁJDÁN

"Komáj" *is* "a thick round bread."
"Komájdun" *is the name for a pot used for keeping* "komáj" *in it.* "Komájdun"
*is also used to describe an unshapely head.*
"Kallaw be komájdun mimune!"  *"His head is like a bread-pot."*
[*etymology*: komáj = kom-áj;

"áj" cf "áw": "ad" = *to eat, as (Sankrit)(also cf* "áj-il", "n-áw-tá", "kark-as"., *(see BQM p.44) also cf* "omáj" = ? om-áj = *a porridge made of flour.*
"kom-", *cf* गुह् guh, *to hide, to cover,* गुप् gup, गुप्त gupta *(Sanskrit)* गुहा guhá, *a cavern, a cave, hiding place, a pit, a hole. Also cf* "ni-gup, *(BQM p.2217) see* "nehoftan" *below.*
*semantic reconstruction: Cf* "xonb", "xomb", "xom" = *a jar;* "kom" = *stomach;* "honb-", "ne-hoftan", *to hide;* "hanbán", "gonbad", "gombad" *(a dome),* "nehanban", "nehonbidan", "anbán".]

## KORK

*The fine nap consisting of fine hairs, on any surface is called* "kork".
"Kork e ru ye holu." *"The fine "fuzz" on the surface of a peach."*
"Hanuz riwew kork-e." *"His beard is not hard and bristly, it is like a fuzz therefore, "he is too young and inexperienced."*
*etymology:* √?

## KORKORI

*This word is almost always used with* "xándan": "korkori xándan", *means to brag about one's abilities, and superiority, and to despise the opponent by singing songs, and citing examples in order to cripple the opponent psychologically. This is done customarily prior to wresting, duels, backgammon and other games, played by two individuals. Thus:*
"Dige bará ye ussát korkori naxuni-há!" *"Don't brag, before your master teacher!"*
[*etymology:* √?*Cf* kor; gerán; goura *(big)(Kurdish); of the same root as* gol, qara, xar, *etc*
गुरू guru; gurvi;*(comparative)* गरीयस् garyas; *(superlative)* गरिष्ट gariwtha
*(Sansk): (1- heavy; weighty. 2- great; large. 3- important; great. 4- arduous; difficult (to bear). 5- great; excessive; 6- violent; heavy; hard of digestion (as food). 7- haughty; proud)*
गौरवं gauravan *(Sanskrit)(1- weight; heaviness. 2- importance)*]

## KOSBARAXAR

[kosbara-xá: kusbara-xá: *(Guilaki, cussword: a worthless landlord)*(Gilaki: downám: xodávand e xáne ye bi-arzew) = kosbara-xá:
*(not related with)*(bastegi nadárad bá): kos; barádar; xáhar

kusbara; kosbara; kozbara *(coriander)*(gewniz);
*(In Iranian culture coriander, is something worthless, used only when there is
no other choice).* "gorbe az gownegi gewniz mixore."*(cat eats coriander when
starving.Persian proverb)*
xá: § xanexá *(landlord; man of the house)*(xodávand e xáne) *cf* xánexázan
*(housewife; woman as the landlord)*
kusbara-xá: *a man, as the landlord or the lord of a worthless and despicable
house.*](JGS)


## KOSMAWANG

*A pejorative term used as a substantive referring to somebody of low
intelligence and frivolous behavior.* "Doxtare ye kosmawang hezár toman
dáde ye dasband xaride." *"The frivolous girl has spent 1000* tomán *on a
bracelet."*
[*etymology:* kos-, *see* kos wer, mawang: √?


## KOS-WER; KOS O WER

absurd; idle talk; nonsense; *yáve; soxan e bihude*
*example:* "Kos-wer nagu!" (Don't say nonsense!). *"Vel kon bábá hamw kos-
wer-e!"* (Leave it alone. It's all nonsense.)
*This term is commonly used with either* "báftan" *or* "goftan". *It is pejorative.*
"Kos-wer/ kos o wer mibáfe." *"He is constantly bull-shitting."*
[*etymology:* kos: k→g→x→q *and* s→w→r→l,
*thus* "kos" *is equivalent of* "ger"; *noted in* "gerán"; "qara"; "qol"
wer: w→s→z→ź
$$\downarrow$$
z→f→v→b
wer *is equivalent of* har-, *in* harak *(Pahlavi);* harz; harze; xarak *(loose; useless)*
*Semantic reconstruction for* "wer": ver; ver-ver *(idle talk);* zer; zer-zer
*(nonsense; saying nonsense);* her; her-her; her zadan; her mizane; herher
mizane; *(rude laughter; laughing without a cause);* her zadan; her mizane;
herher mizane; herri *(get lost!);* xormá-xarak *(a bad date, not edible).*
*Thus* "kos-wer": *great loose talk; big nonsense; colossal stupid talk*
*semantic reconstruction: for* "kos" § gerán.
*note:* kos-wer *is not ralted with* kos, kus *(vulva) and* wer, *is neither related
with Arabic* شعر we-,r *poetry nor* شعر wa-,r *hair.*]

## KOS XOL

*This word is used as a substantive. It can be used for males and females alike.* "Doxtare ye kos xol, xástegárew o rad kard." *"The girl of poor judgment, rejected the man who wooed her."*
[*etymology: See* kos wer, kos = *big,* xol = *crazy.*]

## KOTE

*This term is almost similar to "litter". It is commonly used for dogs, cats, etc.* "Sage haf tá kote karde." *"The dog gave birth to a litter of 7 puppies." When applied to women, it is pejorative and alludes that the so-and-so woman, becomes pregnant and gives birth to too many kids.* "Tázegi báz terekmun zad o bázam kote kard." *"Recently she delivered, and gave birth to another child."*
[*etymology: Cf* kautaka-, *(Avest)* = kucak = *small, little. cf* kote; kudak; kut-áh; kuc-ak, kol]

## KOUDAN

*(dumb, stupid)*
"Pesare ye koudan cáhár sále tu ye yek kelás-e." *"The dumb boy, has flunked the same course for four years in a row."*
[*etymology:* koudan, *cf.* कद *kádá (Sanskrit)(adjective) 1- dumb, 2- ignorant, foolish.*]

## KOULE

"Koule" *is almost always used with* "kaj", *thus* "kaj o koule", *meaning "crooked", bent, "not straight". Thus:*
"Damáqew kaj o koula-s." *"His nose is bent and crooked."*
"Kaj o koule minevise." *"He writes in a crooked fashion."*
[*etymology:* koula = koul-a, = xV́ahl, xal, *cf* kerdu-xála. *Also cf* कुटिलः *kutiláh (Sanskrit): "crooked."*]

## KUFT

"Kuft" *is a pejorative, abusive term basically meaning "syphilis" (a horrible disease, a few decades ago). It can be used synonymous with "Shut up!" In response to questions or statements: one could say:* "Kuft!" *or* "Kuft o kári!" *Meaning: "Hell with you!"*

"Kuft o zahr e már": *may be used synonymous with* "kuft" *as mentioned above, or sometimes used to mean, everything else.* "Har kuft o zahremári bud, dige tamum wod." *"It is all over now, no matter how unpleasant it was!"* *etymology:* √?

## KUFTI

"Kufti" *is used almost synonymous with* "nefrin wode", *"cursed", "damned".* "Máwin e kufti ráh nemiyofte." *"The cursed car won't run."* "Bad kufti-ye." *"He (or she) is really a bad, cursed individual (or thing)."* *etymology:* √?

## KUK

*This word is used as a substantive. Its primary meaning is "being tuned" (for musical instruments.)* "Kuk-e!" *"The instrument is tuned."* "kuk kardan" *1- to tune, to tune up:* "Tár o kuk kard." *"He tuned up the "Tár". 2- To instigate, to cause sedition, to indoctrinate.* "Hey barádarew o kuk kard, tá raft o zad tu ye guw e rayisew." *"He talked his brother into going and giving a slap on the face of his boss." 3-* "Kuk wodan" *to be tuned up.* "Piyáno kuk wode." *"The piano is tuned up."; "kuk wodan": to be compelled to do something by repeatedly being talked into something.* [*etymology:* "kuk" *cf* "kuku", *a bird, coocoo bird. cf* कु *ku 1-* कवते *kavate, to sound. 2-* कुवते *kuváte: to moan, groan, to cry. 3- kauti* कौति *to hum, to coo.*]

## KUL

"Domew o gozáwt ru kulew o dak wod." *"He put his tail on his back and scurried away."* "Behew báyad kuli bedi." *"You must carry him on your back."* "Bacca ro bezár ru kulet." *"Put the child on your back. Carry the child on your back."* [*etymology:* kul √?; *cf* कुलं kulán *(Sanskrit) the front or fore part. cf* "kul": *the upper part of man's back.;* "kule": *a back pack;* "kuli", *carrying someone on one's back.;* "kule-bár"; *a back-pack;* "kawkul", *See* "kawkul."]

# L

## LACAR

"Lacar" *is a substantive. It is used usually to describe people who use abusive language, and obscene words.* "Zanike ye lacar, dahanew ceft-o-bast nadáre."
*"The foul-mouthed woman! Her mouth is not under her control."*
*Also people of indecent behavior or character are called* "lacar."
"Ye namáyew e lacar." *"An obscene show."*
[*etymology*: lacar √?: *cf* lisidan, lis-, *Indo-European base:* * *leiĝ-, to lick.*
*Also cf* lacar, licár, lajan, rixtan, ridan, *see*: "laqve" *cf lecherous*]

## LAGURI

*Either used alone as a substantive or in combination with* "jende", "jende laguri", "doxtare ye laguri" *(a lewd whore). It is a pejorative term.* "laguri" *is applied to women or girls of loose morality.*
[*etymology and semantic reconstruction*: lag-ur-i
-i: *suffix meaning relationship* pedar *(father)*; pedari *(paternal)*
-ur, *is equivalent of* –var: ganjur = ganjvar *(treasurer)*; dastur = dastvar
*(ordinance; command; minister)*; namur = namvar *(damp)*; ranjur = ranjvar =
ranjbar *(sufferer). Thus* –var, *is a sign of possession of a characteristic usually in excess of normal limits.*
lag = laq = riq *from the same root as* "rixtan"; √ *ri (Sanskrit)(to trickle; drop, ooze; flow). Also compare with* "lacar", "laq", "riq"]

## LAJ

"laj kardan" "lajbázi kardan": *Not to pay attention to warnings and doing exactly the thing that one is not supposed to do."*
"Har ce migoft nane, laj mikard." *"Whatever his granny said, he did the opposite."* "Laj nakon, biyá!" *"Don't be stubborn, come on!"*
*etymology: from* "Arabic: laj: *to insist upon a thing, to quarrel obstinately about; to persevere in.*

## LAJJÁRE

*This word is a substantive. It is applied only to a woman, who is quarrelsome, bad-tempered, and uses abusive language.:* "Sar be sar e in lajjáre nazár."

*"Don't argue with this woman, who is bad-tempered and who is foul-mouthed."*
*etymology: Most probably related with "laj". See "laj".*

## LAKKÁTE

*This word is used as a substantive. It is pejorative and refers to a woman, occasionally a girl (not a child), who is barefaced, and loud-mouthed almost a slut, who can make a scandal, upon any aggravation.*
"Zanike ye lakkáte áberu ye má ro bord." *"The slut (woman), scandalized me."*
[*etymology*: √? *Cf* laguri, lacar, laqve]

## LAK O PIS

"Lak o pis" *is applied to anything like skin, paper, fabric etc, discolored in such a way that there are dark and light blotches on it.*
"Az ruzi ke ábestan wode, suratew lak o pis ávorde." *"Since she became pregnant, her face has developed patches of dark and light spots."(Chloasma/melasma)*
[*etymology*: "lak", *is any spot of discoloration darker than the background.* "Pis" *is any spot of discoloration lighter than the background.*
"pisi = *1- vitiligo. 2- leprosy, a cause of skin discoloration.*
lak ≡ laq <√ dagha-, *(Avest)*, dághá-, *(Sanskrit)*, दह् dáh, *to heat.*
pis < paesa *(Avest) –leprosy, vitiligo*]

## LAM

lam dádan
"lam dádan" = *to lean on...*: "Be deraxt lam dád." *"He leaned on the tree."*
[*etymology*: Indoeuropean base* klei-, *to incline, lean, cf ladder, lean, incline.*
आश्रि *á-wri,* शंश्रि; *sán-wri (Sanskrit): to lean on.* निश्रेनि *ni-wre-ni (ladder):* *klei
< *wri*]

## LAMS = LAS

*This is a substantive. Any member of the body eg arms or legs, eyelids etc which becomes faccid and paralyzed due to muscular atonia, is called "lams".*
"Dastew lams-e." *"His hand is floppy, or paralyzed."*
*etymology: lams, see* "loxm", "law".

67

## LANG

"Páw lang-e." *"His leg is limp." "He has a limping leg." "He is lame."*
"Káremun lang mund." *"Our job or work was halted due to the lack of...."*
"Lang-langán miraft." *"He was going hobbling." "He was hobbling along."*
"Má ro lang gozowt." *"He paralyzed or halted our work, by leaving us waiting for him, or for something that he had to provide."*
[*etymology*: lang लंग् *lang (Sanskrit) to limp*

लंगः *langáh (Sanskrit): limp (substantive), lameness.*]

## LANTARÁNI

*This is almost always used with "goftan". It means a statement which does not make any sense and is considered rude.*
"Lantaráni mige!." *"He says nonsense."* "Lantaráni nagu!" *"Don't say bad words!"*
[*etymology*: "Lantaráni" *is directly derived from Arabic* "lan taráni" = *"You can't see me." A reference to an Islamic story according to which the prophet wanted to see the God, but God's answer was* "Lan taráni" *"You can't see me!", thus the slang use, mentioned above.*]

## LAPAR

"Lapar" *almost always used with* "zadan", *means "overflowing, overflow."*
"Lapar zadan" *is used for waving liquids in a vessel, on the verge of overflowing.* "Áb hey lapar mizad." *"The water waved continuously, and was on the verge of pouring out."*
"Zamin larze umad o áb e estaxr lapar mizad." *"During the earthquake the water in the pool, waved and almost poured out."*
[*etymology*: lapar =? lab-par,; lab = lip,; par-, paridan: *to leap, fly; thus* "lapar", *to leap over (overflow) the lip of the vessel.*]

## LAQ

"Dandunew laq wode." *"His tooth has become loose." "His tooth is coming off."*
"Páye ye miz laqq-e." *"The leg of the table is loose."*
*etymology: See* "laqve."

## LAQVE

*This is a noun meaning a disease remarkable, by diarrhea, drooling and generalized lassitude.* "Laqve dáre." *He is sick with* "laqve."
"Laqveyi" *is somebody afflicted with* "laqve." *The term is used to magnify somebody's lean and sickly body and his muscular weakness and slothfulness.* "Mese laqveyiyá mimune." *"He is like those afflicted with* "laqve." *(generalized asthenia)*
[*etymology and semantic reconstruction*: laqve = laq-ve, *cf* laq, riq, liz, lajan, laq, las, lams, loxm. *Cf* raec-, *(Avesta), to evacuate, pour out*; री *ri,* रीयते *riyáte (Sanskrit): 1- to trickle, drip, ooze, 2- to go, move.* रीति *riti (Sanskrit): 1- moving, flowing, 2- motion, 3- river, stream. Cf.* laguri, lacar]

## LAS

*See* "lams".

## LATTE

*Any piece of cloth, usually old, or tattered, used for mopping and cleaning.* "Zamin o latte bezan (bekew)." *"Clean the floor with a mop." (Mop the floor.)*
[*etymology*: latte = latt-e; lat, *a cusp as a valve; one of the two leaflets of a bipartite door.* √?]

## LAVAND

*This word is used as a substantive. It is applied to young and attractive girls or women, who are very sexy and provocative.*
"Doxtar e lavand-e, mixád pesara ro qor bezane." *"The sexy girl is messing with the young man and wants to make him emotionally involved."*
*etymology:* √?

## LAW

law = *1- a carcass 2- very lazy.*
"Tane law" *somebody extremely lazy. Used by itself:* "Tane-law!" *means "You lazy-bone!" (pejorative.)* "Xeyli tane law-e." *"He is awfully lazy."*
"Pesarew ye lawi-ye!" *"His son is a real laggard."*
[*etymology: See* "laqve", laguri, lacar.
*Also cf* "law": lax, laxative, laxare *(Latin)* < laxus = lax, *Late Latin*: *lascare.
Also cf* ललित *lalita (Sanskrit): flabby. Also see*: "loxm".]

## LAZEJ, LEZEJ

*This is an adjective, meaning, "slimy", "gooie". Anything like glue which is sticky, and mucoid is called* "lazej".
"Áb e damáqew lezej-e." *"His nasal discharge is mucoid in character."*
[*etymology: Cf* lazej, lacar, licar, *all cf with* "laqve." *See*: laqve, riq.]

## LÁQ

*This word is almost always used as either* "láq e giset", *when said to a girl or a woman, or* "Láq e riwet", *when applied to a man or a boy. It is depreciative and usually jocular.*
"In áwi ke poxti láq e giset." *"This porridge which you cooked, is worth (good for) your braided hair." The term is used only in referring to something, usually a bad food, or a bad remark made by someone. As "hair" and "beard" were signs of dignity, one understands the logic for their use. Cutting off hair for women, and shaving the beard, for men used to be a sort of harsh punishment, causing disgrace to the victim.*
[*etymology*: "Láq", *is probably derived from Arabic* "láyeq" = *deserving; goof for; proper for.*]

## LÁS

"Lás" *is equivalent of* "flirtation". "lás zadan" = "lásidan" = *to flirt.* "Hamaw bá doxtará miláse." *"He constantly messes with girls." (flirts with them).*
"Hey miláse." *"He constantly flirts."* "Nalás!" *"Stop flirting!"* "Gorbehe bá muwe lás mizane." *"The cat plays with the mouse, and deep down the cat likes this game very much."*
[*etymology*: lás: लस् *lás (Sanskrit): to play, flolic,frolic about, skip about, dance.*]

## LÁT O PÁT

*Also see* "ás o pás". "lát o pát" *means somebody who has lost all his money, and has no financial reserve.* "Lát o pát az qomárxune umad birun." *"He came out of the casino, having lost all his money."*
[*etymology*: "pát" *is most probably a co-word, used to rhyme with* "lát". "Lát" *initially a term used in chess, for a queen, who has lost all the major forces, and has nothing to resist an attack.* √? *cf* लुप्त *lupta*; लुपः *lupa*]

70

## LÁWE

"Láw" *is a carcass.  Also any part of the body badly contused and crushed, is* "láw".  "Láwe" *is a carcass.*  "Law" *was discussed before,  see* "law."
"Máwin zad behew, áw o láwew kard."  *"He hit a car, and was badly crushed."*
"Láwaw o endáxtan tu rudxune."  *"His dead body was disposed of in a river."*
[*etymology: see* "laqve."
*semantic reconstruction*: cf "las": *loose, limp, flaccid*
"law": *very lax, a cadaver*
"láw": *1- cadaver 2- crushed*
"láwe": *a cadaver; the broken body of a car etc?*
"leh": *crushed, and softened, pounded and softened*
"riq": *squeezed and softened.*
"rix" = "riq"
*also:* "liz", "lezej", "lajan", *and* "loxm".]

## LEH

"leh" = *squeezed and softened.*
"Zir e pá lehew kard."  *"He crushed it under his feet."*  *"He trampled it"*
"Leh o lavarde" *means anything badly crushed and bruised.*
"Mizanam leh o lavardat mikonamá!"  *"I warn you! I'll beat the shit out of you!"*
[*etymology*: "leh": *see* "law", *and* "láwe".  "laqve", "lacar", "laguri"
"Lavarde" *past participle of* "lavardan" ≡ "navardan", "navardidan" *(to roll out, to press out as a ball of dough), thus crushed and rolled out.*]

## LEYLEY

"Leyley" *to hop on one foot.* "Baccehá leyley bázi mikonan."  *"The children play a game, by hopping on one leg."*
[*etymology: Cf* "leyley, *with* "lili"
*Cf* ललित *lálita (Sanskrit) – playing, sporting, dallying.  Cf* लीला *lila- a play, sport, amusement.  Also cf* "qáqá-lili", "lili lili houzak, *and* "lili be láláw gozowt."]

## LEK O LEK

"Lek o lek" *almost always used with verbs e.g.* "Kardan", "nevewtan", "raftan" *etc, means,* "very slowly", "sluggishly."

"Xeyli lek o lek mikone." *"He does (it) very slowly"*.
"Lek o lek miraft." *"He was going very slowly." (or sluggishly)*.
[*etymology*: ?; ? lek = laq, √ ri: *see* "laqve"]

## LEMM

*This is a noun. It means knack, a specific and very critical way of handling something, in order to run it efficiently. It may be applied to machines, devices, methods, and ways.*
"Kár kardan e bá in máwin lemm dáre." *"Working with this machine, has a specific method/knack."*
"Lemmew dige dastam umade." *"Already I know how to handle it (in order to run it efficiently)."*
*Etymology: √?*

## LENDEHUR

*This word is used as a substantive.* "Pesar e lendehurew hic honari nadáre." *"His tall boy, is good-for-nothing (has no arts.)"*
"Martike ye lendehur." *"A tall inept man!"*
*This term is pejorative, almost always used referring to males, rarely to females. It has a connotation of tallness, but associated with ineptitude. etymology: √?; Name of a king in ancient India, whose mother became pregnant with him, when the Sun-God (hur = xor =sun) looked at her. land = son (BQM p.1907). [I could not verify land = son](JGS)*
*[etymomogy: ?]*

## LENG

"Leng" *means lower limb, lower extremity. Also it means "thigh, upper thigh",* "Lenget o jamm kon!" *"Remove your legs (lower limb) from my way!"*
"Pesar e leng derázi dáre." *"He has a lanky (long-legged) son." "He has a lanky (long-legged) son."*
"Doxtare leng o pácaw o endáxte birun." *"the girl has exposed her thighs and legs."*
[*etymology: See* "leng o páce"]

## LENG O PÁCE

*Also see* "leng".

"Leng o pace" *is almost synonymous with* "par o pace." *It is commonly used to refer to* "bare legs, and thighs of women or young girls," (par o páce *should mean,* "arms and legs")

"leng o pácaw o endáxte birun." *"She has exposed her thighs and legs."*

"Leng o pace ye xowgeli dáre." *"She has beautiful thighs and legs."*

[*etymology*: páce = pá-ce, pá = *foot, leg;* -ce, *diminutive suffix.*
leng: *Indo-European base\** qleng-, *to bend. Also encountered in German* lenken = *to bend. Old High German:* hlanca = *hip, Anglosaxon:* hlanc, *basic sense* "flexible", *English:* lank.]

## LEZEJ

*See* "lazej"

## LICÁR

*Also see* "lacar".

Licár" *is almost always used with* "goftan". "Licár goftan" *"to use abusive language, to use bad language."* "Cerá licár migi?" *"Why you say bad words?"* "Can tá licár be má endáxt." *"He uttered a few bad word, towards us (me)"*

[*etymology*: "licár", *cf* "lacar", *also see* "laqve:]

## LIFE = NIFE

"Life" *is a noun, referring to tucked-in waist of a pants through which an elastic band is passed.* "Eskenás o tu ye life ye walvárew qáyem kard." *"He hid the paper-money in the* "life" *of his pants."*

*etymology:* √?

## LILI (1)

"Tázegi xeyli lili be láláw mizáre!" *"Recently he/she fawns on him/her to please him/her."* *This idiom* (Lili be lálá ye kasi gozáwtan) *means that somebody treats somebody else in such a way to please him/her, and thus probably to gain his/her favor.*

[*etymology*: ? *Also see*: "leyley".

*cf* लीला lila (Sanskrit): *1- play, sport, pleasure, amusement 2- amorous pastime, or sport.*

लालनं *lálánán: caressing, fondling.*

73

lálá *cf.* लालसा *lálásá: 1- longing or ardent desire 2- the longing of a pregnant woman.*
*Thus:* "Lili be lálá ye kasi gozáwtan" = *to caress or fondle (in order to appease the) longing or desire of somebody.*]

## LILI (2)
*Only in the children's song of* "lili lili houzak" "Gonjiwk e umad áb boxore oftád tu houzak." (*No clear cut meaning is given in the dictionaries for* "lili"): "Lili" *means play, sport, pleasure, amusement. See* "lili" (1)". *Also,* "qáqá lili" *in children's language means* "sweets, and amusement" "qáqá" = *sweets, and* "lili" *see above.*

## LIVIR
*This word is used almost always in referring to thick or hanging lips.*
"Martike ye ikbiri bá labá ye livirew doxtara ro mác máli mikard." "*The despicable man, kissed the girl profusely, with his thick turned-out lips.*"
[*etymology*: livir – liv-ir; -ir, *archaic suffix* < -ivar *cf* "dabir" "liv" = lab., lap-, *(Old Iranian). Also cf.* "laviwe = *an instrument used to roll a camel's lip in order to tame it.* labe = *flap*; raf = *a shelf. But not* "laváw" (*A sort of bread, most probably* lav-áw, *cf* áw, √ ad = *to eat, essen, cf* karkas, = kark-as, (*a vulture = an eating bird*) (*BQM, see* "áw")]

## LIZ
*slippery*
"Bárun umad, zaminá liz wod." "*It rained, and the pavements became slippery.*"
*etymology: See* "lezej, laq, laqve, riq".

## LOMBAR
"Lombar" *means plump or fat buttock(s).*
"Doxtare lombará ye gondaw o endáxte birun, xábide tu áftáb." "*The girl has exposed her fat buttocks to the sun.*"
[*etymology: See* "áblambu." *Also: cf* लंब *lamba (adj): 1- hanging down or from, pendent, dangling, hanging upon, 2- great, large. Cf* लंब् *lámb,* लंबते *lámbáte (Sanskrit) 1- to hang down, hang from, dangle, 2- to be attached, hold on to*]

74

## LOND-LOND

*This term is used synonymous with* "qor-qor", *meaning,* "grumbling." " lond = Lond-londew man o be jun ávorde." *"His constant grumbling (nagging/complaining), is killing me."*
*etymology: ?*

## LONG

*This term means a loincloth. Also a thin checkered colorful cotton sheet used by men to cover the lower part of the body in the public bath-houses.*
long endáxtan: *to submit to defeat.*
"Bábá long endáxt." *"The guy submitted to defeat, yielded to the superiority of the opponent."*
*etymology:* long < *langotha, langoth (Hindi) (BQM p1908)*

## LOXM

*This is an adjective, used only when referring to* "a boneless meat".
"Yek kilu guwt e loxm bede." *"Give me one kilo of boneless meat."*
*etymology: See*; laqve, riq, law, láw.

## LOPP

"Lopp" *is the slang equivalent of* "gune" *or* "cheek".
"Loppáw gol endáxte." *"Her cheeks blushed."*
"Do loppi mixord." *"He was eating with both cheeks bulging."*
[*etymology: Cf* लपनं *lapanan (mouth of animal beings.), cf* लप् *láp,* लपति *lápáti (to speak, talk.)*]

## LOPPI

*Also see* "lopp".
"Loppi" *is almost always used as:* "Ewtebáh e loppi." *"A blunder", "A big mistake."*
*etymology: See* "lopp".

## LOU

*Always used with* "dádan", *means, to betray, to expose someone's secrets.*
"Dustew o lou dád." *"He betrayed his friend." "He exposed the secret of his friend."*
"Man o lou nadiyá.!" *"Don't you dare betray me!"*

*etymology*: "lou"? *"to say, speak". See* "lopp".

## LOUDE

*This is a substantive. It is referred to a man or woman, whose social behavior is liked by his or her friends, primarily because he or she does things, or makes remarks which are hilarious, witty and funny.*

"Az dast e doxtare ye loude rudebor wodim." *"(literally) We burst with laughter by the funny girl."*

[*eymology*: loude = ? lou-de,: lou, *see* "lou": *and* -de, < dádan,; "lou dádan" *"to expose people's secrets,* "lou-de" *"one who exposes secrets of the people, and thus causes fun."*]

## LUC

*This is a substantive, meaning "cross-eyed", "affected with strabismus."*
"Luc-e." *"He is cross-eyed."*
[*etymology: ? Cf "Louche" (French), "luscus" (Latin).*]

## LUL = VUL

1- lul = vul: "Vul nazan!" "= Lul nazan!" *"Don't wiggle!"* "vul zadan" = "lul zadan" = "lulidan" = *"to wiggle, to squirm."* "Cerá hamaw miluli?" *"Why you are constantly wiggling?"*

2- "lul wodan": *to become dizzy and delightful. To become high on drugs.* "Do bast zad lule lul wod!" *"He took two joints, and became high."* "lul kardan" = *to make dizzy and delightful, to make high* "lul" = *high, dizzy and delightful.*

[*etymology: Cf* लोल *lolá: (Sanskrit) 1- shaking, rolling, moving to and fro, dangling. 2- agitated, restless, uneasy.* लुल् *lul,* लोलित *lolita;* लोलति *loláti,* लुलित *lulita (Sanskrit)(lulide): 1- to roll (about), toss about, move to and fro. 2- to shake, stir, disturb.*]

## LULU

*A bugbear, is used when one wants to scare children.* "Lulu" *is* "any monstrous creature", *in children's language.*
"Gerye nakon, lulu miyád." *"Don't cry, the bugbear will come."*
[*etymology:* lulu = lul-u, -u, *a suffix of exaggeration, in unpleasant things. Cf* "riw-u", "riq-u", "guz-u" *etc.*; lul, *see* "lul". *Thus* "lulu" *is someone, or a creature who disturbs, causes agitation, and disorder.*]

## LUS

*This is a substantive. It refers to anybody or anything insipid, lacking good taste.*

"Namáyew e lusi bud." *" The show was quite insipid."*

"Ce lus! = Ce xonak!" *"How insipid! Such poor taste.!"*

"Xodet o lus nakon!" *"Don't make insipid gestures or remarks, thus, you cannot gain favor by these gestures or remarks."*

*etymology:* √?

# M

## MACAL

*This term is almost always used with* "kardan" *or* "wodan". "Macal kardan" *(vt) or* "macal wodan" *(vi),* "macal" *is the state of somebody who is disappointed and ashamed (embarrassed).*
"Didi ce juri má ro macal kard.?" *"did you see how he embarrassed me?"*
"Jelo ye dustáw macalew kard." *"He was disappointed and put to shame in the presence of his friends."*
*etymology:* √?

## MAME

"Mame" *means* "bossom, breast"; *usually beautiful, young breasts are called* "mame." *Also* "mame" *is sometimes used instead of* "breast-feeding".
"Biyá junam mame boxor." *"Come on dear, let me breast-feed you."*
"Mamehá ye xowgelew mes e limu mimune." *"Her beautiful breasts are like lemons."*
[*etymology*: "mame", *cf mamma (Latin): mother, breast*; má (Sanskrit) mother. mammi, *mastos (Greek) (breast.)* मा *má (Sanskrit) 1- a mother, 2- the Goddess of wealth, Lakshmi.*]

## MANGUL

*Also see* "wangul", *and* "mast-o-malang"
"Mangul" *is the name of some characters in folktales.*
*etymology: See and cf* "malang", "mast o malang" *and* "wangul".

## MANTAR

*This is substantive. It refers to someone's treatment of a subject, or approach to a problem, quite enigmatic and confounding, causing perplexity and dismay.*
"Bebin bacce ye ye vajabi ce jur má ro dah máh e ázegár antar mantar karde."
*"See how this young lad (a midget child) has perplexed us and has kept us in a state of confusion and undecidedness for a full 10-month period."*
[*etymology*: antar: *ape (folk etymology)*
antar: ≡ *andar. antra (Sanskrit)(in, inside, within)*

78

"mantar": mánsr, *(Pahlavi): divine inspiration, God's word. Mantra (Avest) =*
*God's word, God's message. "Mantran" (Avest) = prophet, carrier of the*
*God's message. <man = to think, मन् (Sanskrit)(BF p.358). Thus, involved in a*
*mantra, not being able to figure out the situation]*

## MAST O MALANG

*This term describes the state of people who live in abundance and bliss,*
*oblivious to the dangers and miseries of life ( in their immediate or distant*
*environment). "Baccehá mast-o-malang, qaltezan, wádi yo bázi yo jahewhá*
*kardand." "The cubs, drunk with bliss and happiness rolled, made cheers and*
*frolicked."*
[*etymology*: mast: √ madha-, *(Avest); intoxicating, mattá (Sanskrit) =*
*intoxicated, मद् mád (Sanskrit): to revel or delight in, to intoxicate, to inebriate.*
malang, *cf* "wangul" *and* "mangul": मंगल *mángálá (Sanskrit) 1- auspicious,*
*lucky, propitious, 2- prosperous, doing or faring well.*]

## MATAL

*See* "atal".

## MAWDI, MAWTI

*This word is a title referring both to men and women. It apparently originates*
*from the name of the holy city of Mash-had, where one of the Imams of Islam is*
*buried. A man or woman who has successfully made a pilgrimage to "Mash-*
*had" (Meshed), is thus called by the title of "Mash-hadi" or "Mashdi". "Mawti*
Ebád" "*Mr.* Ebád"
"Mawti xánum ámad." "*The lady or Mrs... came.*"
[*etymology: vide supra. also see* "Kabláyi" *cf* mawt *(full, rich).*
*This etymology may be erroneous. An alternative explanation must take into*
*consideration that the name of many terms and villages in post-Islam era were*
*wrongly spelled and manipulated by ignorant scribes who tried to find Arabic*
*homophonic words with the Persian terms which did not make any sense to*
*them. Examples:* tayyebát *instead of* taibád; ráhatábád *instead of* rahtábád *or*
rahtáván; *Mashad (Arabic place of martyrdom) may well be a similar error.*
*The true name being* Mawat *or* Mawtáván *derived from* mawt *(full, rich,*
*flourishing, prosperous). Thus the town of prosperity.*]

## MÁC

"mác", *a noun, means a kiss*, "Labáw o mác kard." *"He kissed her lips."*
"Ye mác e ábdár" *"A juicy kiss."*
[*etymology: See* mus mus". "mazidan" *(to suck)*]

## MÁFANGI

*See* "mofangi"

## MESMES

"Mesmes" *is synonymous with* "fesfes". *It is used with* "kardan".
*Thus:*"mesmes kardan" *= to do or perform very slowly, to procrastinate.
Dawdle; dilly dally.*
"Candán mesmes o fesfes kardand tá yáru mord." *"They procrastinated so
much, until, the (poor) man died."*
*etymology: ?*

## MEZQUN

mezqun = *1- music, 2- Musical instrument esp. a fiddle, or any stringed
instrument.* "Mezqun mizane". *"He plays music, He plays a musical stringed
instrument."*
"To ham mezqunci wodi?" *"(depreciative): "You have become a fiddler too?"*
[*etymology*: "mezqun" < *mousiki (Greek).* = music. *also* "mescal" = mezqun =
*music. mousiki (tekni)(Greek), musical art originally an art of the Muses <
mousa = a Muse.*]

## MOFANGI = MÁFANGI

*This is a substantive.* Mofangi *means sickly, puny, easily damageable, prone
to illness and disease.*
*etymology*: mofang, mofan, +u, or +i:
*-i is a suffix denoting possession of a quality.*
[mofang: *compare with* "mof" *nasal discharge. Thus* "mofang-i" *or*
"mofangu" *means* "one whose nasal discharge is copious, and by extension
always sick or having cold".]

## MOFT(I)

*1- free of charge, 2- absurd, nonsense,* "moft", *and* "mufti" *are used
interchangeably as an adjective or adverb.* "Xunaw o moft foruxt." *"He sold*

his house for nothing (very cheap)." "In ketáb o mofti behem dád." *"He gave me this book for free."* "Harf e moft nazan!" *"Don't say nonsense.!"* [*etymology*: "mofti" *an Arabic word, which means someone who gives a decisive response* "أفتى" *aftá, to judge, give a judicial decision. To give a verdict of sacred law or a legal opinion. Thus an interpreter or expounder of religious law in certain Islamic countries. Thus "mufti" meaning "given for free" or "free of charge" alludes to the depreciation of the Islamic justice thus administered by religious judges. Also "nonsense", the figurative meaning, alludes to the public opinion about the administration of law by the "moftis".*]

## MOK

"Mok" *means, exactly; with no deductions or discount.*
"Mok dah tumán." *"Ten tuman exactly, with no discounts whatsoever."*
"Mok sad tumán gereft." *"He charged exactly 100 tomans, no more and no less."*
*etymology:* √?

## MOSAMMÁ

1- "Mosammá" *is almost always used in conjunction with other words, such as* "kadu" *(squash),* "álu" *(prune), etc. Thus* "álu mosammá", *is the name of a Persian dish, made with prune, meat and vegetables.*
"Diwab álu-mosammá xordim." *"Last night we had* "álu-mosamma"."
*etymology:* √?

2- bi mosammá: *1- empty. 2- ineffective. 3- powerless*
Kárfarmá wod ammá bimosammá. *He is the worker-troop leader- but this position is devoid of executive power.*

## MUL

"Mul" *is used as a noun. It refers to an illicit sexual partner or pronoun, usually a male.*
"Zanike mulew o ávord tu xune tu ye ganje qáyem kard." *"The woman brought her paramour into the house and hid him in a closet."*
"Doxtare engár mul karde." *"It seems as though the girl, has had an illicit sexual partner." This use is particular to the Guilaki dialect.* "mul kardan" = *to have illicit sexual relation with a man.*
*etymology:* √?

## MUSMUS

"musmus" = *To follow somebody with an ingratiating manner; To follow especially for a male dog, a bitch, and smell and lick the bitch's external genitalia.*

"Martike oftáde donbál e zan e mardom, musmus mikone!"  *"The despicable man is wooing somebody else's wife."*

[*etymology: Semantic reconstruction: cf* mus; maz; mak; makidan; mác; muc. *basic concept; to suck.* mác, *cf* mik, mak.

micitan *(Pahlavi)(to suck). dialcects:* mik, mic √ * meq, *or* √ mec (makidan)*(to suck)(BQM p.2002)*]

# N

**NANU**

"Nanu" *or* "na-nu", *is a noun, meaning a hammock,* "Bacca ro gozowt tu nanu o raft." *"She put the infant in the hammock and left."*
*etymology:* √?

**NATARBUQ**

"Natarbuq" *is a substantive, meaning tall, corpulent, boorish man.*
Martike ye natarbuq umade az nanaw pul mixád. *The husky, rude man asks his granny for money.*
*etymology:* natarbuq: náder beyg; náder alladingh. *The tyrant King Nader and* buq *pejorative of* beyg.

**NAWV O NEMÁ**

*This term means* "growth and development. *"It is commonly used with* "kardan" *thus,* "nawv o nemá kardan" = *to grow and develop.* "Yáqiyá dar sarásar e kewvar nawv o nemá kardand." *"The rebels appeared in every part of the country."*
*etymology:* "nawv" *from Arabic* نشو nawv: *to grow, develop.*
"nemá" < "nemudan" *to show, figuratively* "to wax", "to increase."

**NÁ**

"Ná" *is almost always used as* "ná nadáwtan": *not to have any strength, to be exhausted.*
"Ná nadáre ráh bere." *"He has no stamina (strength) to walk."*
"Mage nun naxordi ke ná nadári?" *"Have you had no bread, that you lack strength?"*
*etymology:* √?

**NÁKAS, NÁKES**

*This is a substantive. Meaning: ignoble, vice, mean, knavish, of bad character.*
*example:* "Xeyli nákes-e." *(He is a vicious man. He is ignoble. He is mean.)*
"Nákes man o tanhá gozowt." *(the rogue left me alone in a difficult situation.)*

*[etymology and semantic reconstruction: In contrast to general belief, "nákas"
is not made of "ná-," (privative prefix) and "kas". I believe "nákas" was
originally "nák-kas", with omission of one "k" "nákas" is formed. "nák" was
frequently used in Pahlavi language, eg "anák" (1- bad; mal-,; vicious; wicked
2- mixed; impure)*
*Along the same line of reasoning: nák-kám → nákám nák-kerdár → nákerdár;
nák-manew; nákravew; náktoxme; cf naughty (English). also cf náqolá <
\*nák-koláh (ill-bred); ná-qolá (someone with stigma of mischievousness or of
wicked breed); náqes (?Arabic loanword); (defective); naqs (?Arabic
loanword)(defect); najes (?Arabic loanword)(filthy; dirty); and nákojá and
nákojá-ábád (A remote desolate place where nobody visits). Again I believe
nákojá = nák-kojá (with omission of one "k") or "nák-já" (a wicked or bad
place).]*

## NÁQ

*Almost always used as "tá náq"* "up to the nose", "up to the brim", "up to the
throat".
"Tá náqew por kard." *"He filled it up to the brim."*
"Tá náqew xorde." *"He has overeaten. He has had his fill of...."*
"Tá náqew tapunde." *"He has filled it up, or crammed it."*
*[etymology: náq? cf :* नासाच *násá (Sanskrit) a nose. cf. náy*

*náq? Cf nouk, nox:* मुख *mukhá: 1- mouth 2- snout, muzzle. See noxále.]*

## NÁQOLÁ

*This is a substantive. It means somebody who is shrewd, who can easily take
one in on dealings.*
"Rubáh e náqolá, morqa ro gul zad o gardanew o gereft." *"The cunning fox,
deceived the hen and snatched the hen's neck."*
*[etymology: náqolá = ná-qolá: mak-nákkoláh; mák, nák (bad, wicked, ill)
alternatively, ná-, privative prefix; qolá = kola cf "kákol". Basic concept:
"koláh", a sign of good-birth: Thus "náqolá ": of ill-birth, ignoble or not well-
born, not wearing the sign of noble birth. (In certain parts of Iran not wearing
a hat, is a sign of dishonor for a man. By "hat", one means any sort of "head-
gear")]*

## NÁSUR

*This is an adjective, meaning "chafed; macerated". "Angowtam násur wode."*
*(My finger is macerated.)*
[*etymology*: ná-sur, ná = aná-, *(privative prefix) and* "sur" *compare with* "zur"
*(power, force, strength);* zuhr *(Pahlavi),* závar *(Avest):* sura *(Avest)(powerful);*
asura *(Avest)(weak; incompetent); compare with:* "zevár", "zevár-dar-rafte",
"qamsur" (= kamzur) *(broken; fallen; weak, etc)*]

## NÁTOU

*This is a substantive. It means somebody who is hard to deal with.*
"Ádam e nátouyiye, hic jur nemiwe báháw kenár umad." *"He is very hard to*
*deal with. One cannot come to terms with him in any way."*
[*etymology*: nátou = ?ná-tou: ná-, *privative prefix;* tou < táb: *to swing, to flex,*
*to bend, to warp; thus* ná-tou = *inflexible.*]

## NÁWI

*This is a substantive, meaning somebody who is not an expert is a craft or*
*trade, and thus prone to errors.*
"Ránande ye náwi." *"An inexperienced driver."*
"Jarráh e náwi." *"an inexperienced surgeon."*
"Bábá xeyli náwiye." *"He is awfully inexperienced."*
[*etymology*: náwi = ná-aw-i: ná-, *privative prefix;* aw-, awá = *completeness or*
*perfectness in character or deeds,* awá = ard, arta, areta *(Avest);* rita ऋत
*(Sanskrit)(proper, right) ; thus:* ná-w-i: *somebody who is not perfect in a craft*
*or skill. Cf :* wá-gerd *(one who practices in order to acquire* "awá" *in a skill or*
*craft.);* aw-u; awáyi; Ardawir; Ardabil, *etc.*]

## NÁZ

1- *vulva: See* "nos", *cf* "nos", *and* "xornás", *and* "now-xár".
2- "náz", *and* "náz kardan": *This term is used when somebody is offered*
   *something or an opportunity. Although one likes to have it, however one*
   *declines to accept it, only to be "coerced" into accepting it.*
"De náz nakon, begir." *"Come on now! Take it."*
"Doxtre xeyli náz dáre." *"This girl although likes....but does not show overt*
*signs of eagerness."*
*etymology: See* "nos".

## NEFLE

1- *As an interjection* "nefle!". *It is addressed to people, whom one wants to despise as worthless.*

2- *Used with* "wodan": "Nefle wodan", *means* "to be wasted"; "to be ruined; :to be destroyed". "Nefle kardan", *is* "to waste, ruin, destroy."
"Hame ye sarmáyaw nefle wod." *"his capital resources were wasted."*
"Bábá ro nefle kard." *"He ruined, or destroyed the fellow.", "He killed him."*

[*etymology:* nefle = nefl-e; nefl ≡ nefr: < nefridan = *to curse: ne-, privative prefix*; fri-d-an < áfrivana *(Avest)(blessing) (BQM p.51)*]

## NEQ, NEQNEQ

"Neq (neq-neq) zadan": *to nag; nagging.*
"Hey neq neq zad, xafam kard." *"He nagged me to death."*
*etymology:* √?

## NIFE

*See* "life"

## NINI

*This is a noun, used when talking with young children or infants. It means* "an infant", "a baby."
"Nini ro bebin." *"See the baby."*
"Biyá nini xerse mame boxor." *"literal: Come on you big-bear-baby, suck the breast." (This is addressed to older children or adults, who behave very immaturely.")*
*etymology:* √?

## NO(U)KAR

*This is a substantive. meaning* "servant", "waiter".
*example:* "Noukar e man-e. *"He is my servant. He is my slave."*
[*etymology:* nou-kar, nou ? < nev-ak, neva-en *(Pahlavi)(good; fine)*; nev́ *(Pahlavi)(brave; good); and* "kar" *most probably derived from* √ kr; kereta-, kerenaoite *(Avest)(to make; to do); Thus* "nou-kar" *(one who carries out works in a good manner.)*]

## NONOR

*This is a substantive. It is applied to somebody who does stupid, and childish things to endear himself for somebody else.*

"De boro xodet o nonor nakon!" *"Now, off with you! Stop your nonsense childish behavior (You can't make yourself loved this way.)"*

"Doxtare xeyli nonore. Umad newest ru zánu ye marde, hey busew kard." *"The girl is awfully "nonor", sissy she sat on his lap and started kissing him."*
*etymology:* √?

## NOS

*infantile vulva.*

"Be kosam, be nim nosam!" *"A pejorative, depreciative remark, meaning "so-and-so, or whatever happened is not worth a farthing (is not worth half of my vulva.)"*

[*etymology:* nos ≡ now ≡ náz; nowxár, xornás.
*Basically "nose" (English) from Sanskrit:* नासा. *Násá: nose (English), trunk of an elephant.* "nos" *infantile vulva. Cf* "now-xár" *(to ruminate), eating with the mouth closed.), see* "xornás, *and* "náz".]

## NOUCE

"Nouce" *is a substantive. It is almost synonymous with "novice" or "neophyte".* "Ci migi nouce?" *"What you want, you neophyte?"*

"Az noucehá ye do morwed yeki umad jelou." *"One of the young disciples of the spiritual leader came forth."*

[*etymology:* "nouce" = nou-ce: -ce, *a diminutive suffix;* nou *(new)* < nava-, *(Avest)(new);* nává नव *(new).*]

## NOXÁLE

*This is a substantive, meaning:*

1- *The big, coarse uneven clumps of dried mud, flour, etc. Coarse, sharp pieces of rock.*

2- *Somebody who is rude and coarse in his manners. Somebody with abrasive personality.*

"Hame ye noxále ye qand o rixt birun." *"He discarded all the coarse clumps of sugar."*

"Pesare xeyli noxálas, xodet o beppá." *"The fellow is very rude, take care of yourself."*

[*etymology*: noxále = nox-ál-e: nox: < मुख *mukhán (Sanskrit): face, snout, the front or forepart, the tip, point.*
*Semantic reconstruction: cf* nox; nouk *(bill, beak, tip, sharp end);* nox-ri *(first-born, evacuated first);* nox-ráz, nox-rás *(pioneer);* nox-ost (*nox-est) (?) *(first);* noxále *(jagged, ie anything with pointed, sharp ends or sides.)*]

# O

## OMMOL

*Only used in reference to people, referring to their customs and weltanschauung, meaning old-fashioned, conservative.*
"Zanew xeyli ommol-e." *"His wife is extremely fanatic, and unsophisticated."*
*etymology:* √?

## ORDANG

*This is a kick given into the rear end of someone or an animal.*
"Ordangi be man zad, kamaram wol wode." *(a folk song) "He kicked me in the ass, I became impotent."*
*etymology:* √?

## OSS

*This is a noun. It is almost always used in conjunction with the Arabic word* "asás": "Oss o asás" *means the fundament, the foundation.*
"Oss o asás e kár o midune." *"He knows the fundamental aspects of the work."*
etymology: Oss *cf* "ostoxán" ast-axv-an.
[*semantic reconstruction*: ast; istádan; ost-ovár, hast, hastu; xostu; xastu; haste; ostováne; √ st; ast-, (Avest) ; *asthi-, (Sanskrit)* अस्थ *ásthi = bone.*]

## OXT

"Oxt gereftan" *is the only form in which* "oxt" *is used.* "oxt wodan" *is rarely used. It means to get used to someone due to long or frequent association.*
"Bá ham oxt-an." *"They are close friends."*
"Bá ham oxt wodan." "Bá ham oxt gereftand(d)." *"They have become bosom friends."*
*etymology:* oxt = ? ox-t, -t, *archaic suffix, e.g.* dus-t, das-t;
[ox-, *cf* haxá *(Old Persian) = friend,* haxá-manew = *of friendly nature or personality. (Achemenides). Cf* सख *sakhá (Sanskrit) = friend.*]

## OZGAL

*(ugly; of grotesque facies or appearance)*

89

*This is a pejorative term, used for degrading somebody. It is more frequently used for men and sometimes for women with ugly face and grotesque appearance.*

*example:* "Ozgal boro gomwo!" *(Get lost you boorish man!).*

*[etymology:? The following derivation is hypothetical.*

"ozgal" *could easily be converted to* "uyqur" *(uyghur), by replacing consonants and vowels, of the same category. If this assumption is correct, then* "ozgal = uyqur", *applies to the Turks of eastern Asia. The appearance, facial features and manners of these foreign invaders were apparently detested by the local people.](JGS)*

# P

## PAKAR

"Pakar" *is a substantive.  It is used when referring to someone who is depressed and disappointed due to unfulfilled wishes.*
"Umad numzadew o bebine, ammá doxtare xune nabud, yáru xeyli pakar wod." *"He came to visit his fiancée, but she was not at home.  He became very depressed and disappointed."*
[*etymology*: √?? paiti-kar-,]

## PAK O PAHLU

*Also compare with* "dak o puz", "dak o dahan", "dak o dande:"
"Zad pak o pahluw o leh kard." *"He beat him hard on his flanks."*
pak: ?
*etymology: ?*

## PANCAR

"Pancar" *means a "flat tire".* "Pancari" *is a hole in a tire.*
"pancar wodan": *1- to become flat (for a tire) 2- to be exhausted or unable to work, or to perform.*
"pancar kardan": *to make a tire flat.*
"Máwinam pancar wod." *"My car had a flat tire."*
"Cerá pancar wodi?" *"Why did you stop working all of a sudden?"*
[*etymology and semantic reconstruction: cf* pancar, panjar, panjar-e (panj-jara); calan, zereh, jouwan.  *All cf* जालं *jálán (Sanskrit): a lattice, a coat of mail.  Also cf* "nánepanjere" *a sort of paper-thin cookie with several holes in it.*]

## PAPU

*This is a substantive.  It refers to somebody who cannot defend his rights and submits easily to those who exploit him.* "Gomán nakon papu-e, xeyli ham zebele ammá ru nemikone." *"Don't think that he is a black sheep, (on the contrary) he is very smart, but he does not exteriorize (his smartness)."*
[*etymology*: papu = pap-u, *suffix, cf* guzu, riwu, gandu, riqu *etc.* "pap" = ? pof. *Cf* "bád" – *swelling, air?*]

91

## PAR O PÁCE

*See* "leng o páce".

[*etymology*: par = *feather, wing; arm; bare arms.*

"par", par *(Pahlavi) wing, feather,* parena-, *(Avest) = feather, wing.* पर्ण *párnán (Sanskrit).* bál *(Guilaki dialect) = arm,* bál *(Lori dialect) = sleeve.*]

## PARSE

"Parse" *means roaming around aimlessly.*

"parse zadan": *to roam around aimlessly, to loiter.*

"To ke hamaw tu xiyábuná parse mizani, key be káret miresi?" *"You are constantly roaming around, when do you get to your work?"*

*etymology:* √?

## PART

*Also see* "cart o part".

1- "part kardan": *to throw, toss away, fling.* "part wodan": *to be thrown, to be tossed.*

2- "part goftan: *to say nonsense.*

3- "part o palá": *scattered; nonsense*

"Hame ye xánevádaw part o palá wodan." *"All members of his family were scattered, (in various parts of the world)"*

4- "havás parti": *confusion, flight of ideas.* "Havás parti dáre = havásew part-e" *"He is confused" "He has flight of ideas."*

## PATE

"Pate ro be áb dádan." *"To divulge a secret."*

"Pataw ru áb oftád." *"Her secret was exposed."*

"Pate" *is a voucher, a ticket or any token authorizing the holder to a certain right.*

"Pataw o váz karde neweste var e divár, del dáde qolve gerefte."

*"She was sitting by the wall, completely relaxed, and extending her legs and she was chatting (with her friends)."*

[*etymology*: < पट्ट: *páttáh (Sanskrit) 1- a slab, tablet for writing upon, a plate in general, 2- a royal grant or edict.*]

## PATE XOLE

1- Pate xole dim dám.": *This is used to describe the face of an awfully ugly individual.*

  pat = pet *(lori)* = *nose*

  xol, xal = xv́ahl = *crooked*

  dim (*see* "dak o dim), = *face*

  dám ≡ taxm, *also cf,* damaq, dam dame. < तामस *tamas (Sanskrit)* = *dark.*

  *thus:* "pate xole dim dám": *someone with crooked nose and dark face.*

2- "pate xole": *This is used to describe a surface (especially the skin of face), with pock marks, and remarkable unevenness.*

[*etymology:* pate = pat-e ? पत् *pát (Sanskrit); to fall.*]

## PATI

"Pati" *is used as a substantive. It is considered to be synonymous with* "nude", *or* "bare", *or* "naked". *Two forms are in common use:*

1- "loxt o pati": "doxtará loxt o pati kenár e áb válibál bázi mikardan." *"The nude girls were busy playing volleyball at the beach."*

2- "pápati": *barefooted:* "Pápati umad xune." *"He came home barefooted."* "Pezewkán e pápati ye Cin" *"The bare-foot doctors of China."*

[*etymology: The combination of* "pati" *with* "loxt" *in* "loxt o pati", *makes me very suspicious that the true meaning of* "pati" *may not be* "bare". *Why repetition of* "Nude" *two times, in the form of* "loxt" *and* "pati" ? *etymology:* √?]

## PAT O PAHN

"pat o pahn" *fallen, spread out and wide.*

"Dahanew xeyli pat o pahn-e." *"Her mouth is too wide."*

"Pat o pahn neweste." *"She is sitting all spread out."*

[*etymology:* "pat" *cf* "fatt-o-farávun": pat. *see* "fatt" #4. *also cf.* "pát", "pátál"]

## PAXME

"paxme" *is almost synonymous with* "papu". *See* "papu".

"Xeyli paxma-s." *"He is awfully submissive." "He is very helpless."*

"Paxme nabáw, boro pullet o bessun!" *"Don't be helpless/submissive, go and get your money."*

"paxme" = paxm-a; paxm = *most probably* "pax-m", *cf.* taxm < *támás* पामर *(dark)*

[pax-m, < *pámás: *cf.* पामरः *pámárá (adj): 1- poor, helpless, 2- foolish, stupid.; cf.* पामरः *pámárá: a fool, an idiot.*]

## PÁCE

1- *Specifically the legs of lamb or sheep used as a special dish.* "Kalle pace mixori?" *"Do you eat the dish made of sheep or lamb head and legs?" (Mutton head and legs.)*

2- *Mostly used with* "leng" *or* "par": *see* "leng o páce", *(bare legs and thighs), and* "par o pace" *(Bare arms and legs.)*

"Rafte leng o pace ye doxtará ro kenár e daryá did bezane." *"He is gone to the beach to ogle the girls' bare legs and thighs."*

[*etymology*: páce = pá-ce: -ce, *diminutive suffix*; pá < pádha *(Avest):* पाद्:: *pádáh (Sanskrit) = foot, leg.*]

## PÁLUN

"Pálán" *or* "pálun" *is a cloth (stuffed) saddle with or without two packs attached to it on either side.*

"Xare hamun xare, pálunew avaz wode." *"It is the same (old) donkey, only its pack-saddle is new." (He has not changed and he is not any better, after education or a course or some training. His exterior has changed, but no change in character). (The situation is basically the same, there is only superficial change.)*

[*etymology*: pálán = pál-án, *cf* pálár:? < bálá <bereza-. (Avest) *or* ? < bar (*Old Iranian*); भर् bhar, भृ bhri (*Sanskrit*); *to carry*]

## PÁT

"Pát" *in chess = stalemate.*

"Lát o pát", *is a substantive, meaning somebody who has lost all his possessions and is totally penniless.*

"Hey qomár kard tá lát o pát/ás o pás wod." *"He gambled so much until he eventually became penniless and lost everything."*

*etymology*: pát < √ पत् *pát (Sanskrit): 1- to fall (down); 2- to fall (in a moral sense) forfeit one's rank or position off. 3- To fall, be reduced to wretchedness* or misery. 4- to go down into hell, go to perdition. *Also cf* : "fatt o farávun", "pat o pahn".

## PÁTIL

"Pátil" *is a big metallic pail or cauldron. In slang* "pátil" *or* "pátil wodan*" means to be extremely drunk and inebriated.* "Bábá umad xune, pátile pátil bud." *"The fellow came home, he was badly drunk."*
[*etymology*: patil = ? pát-il, pát < पत् *pát (Sanskrit) see* "pát."]

## PÁTOQ

"Pátoq" *is a noun. It means a gathering place. Also it means a place where one visits frequently.* "Age xune nis, boro qahve xune, pátoqew unjá-s." *"If he is not at home, go to the coffee shop, his station is there."*
"Pátoq e qomárbázá tu in xuna-s." *"The meeting-place of the gamblers is (in) this house."*
*etymology:* √ ?

## PELEKIDAN

*To go around and tinker with trifling things. To loiter; move around. To be busy with nothing.*
"Xob, ce kár mikoni?" *"Now (tell me) what you do?"* "Ey, mipelekim!"
*"Oh! So-so, I go around and do a little of this and a little of that."*
[*etymology*: pelekidan, = pelek-id-an, *also cf* "telek o pelek": "pelek" *cf* पेल् *pel*, पलति *palate (Sanskrit) = to go, to move.*]

## PESK

"Pesk" *means, small, minuscule. Any meager amount.*
*etymology: See* "pewk".

## PEWK

"Pewk andáxtan", *"to determine by lottery."*
"Pewk mindázim, be har ki oftád, bere az cewme áb biyáre." *"Let's determine by lottery. He who is chosen by lottery, must fetch water from the spring."*
[*etymology: cf* pewkel, *cf* pesk.]

## PILE KARDAN

"Pile" *is a* "tumor", "a boil", a "furuncle". *See* pewk.

"Dandunew pile karde." *"He's got a dental abscess." "He has a gumboil."*
"Pase sarew dewpel dáre." *"He has got a tumor on the back of his neck."*
*Figuratively* "Pile kardan" = *to be stubborn and relentless and persevering in having something in one's own way (alluding to a tumor not easily curable.)*
"Pile karde (mixád) bere sinemá." *"He is adamant in his wish to go to the movies."*
"pile" *a cocoon.* "Kerm e abriwom pile baste." *"The silk worm made a cocoon."*
[*etymology and semantic reconstruction*: pil, pel, pile, a *tumor, a boil. Basically "a small round ball-like object". pila (Latin) = a ball, cf* pewk, pewkel, pesk, dowpel, dewpel, doźpel *(a malignant tumor)*]

## PINAKI

"Pinaki" *is a nap.* "pinaki zadan" = *to take a nap.* "Pas az náhár pinaki zadim." *"After lunch, we took a nap."*
*etymology:* √?

## PINE

"Pine" *is a callus, callosity.* "Dastáw pine baste." *"His hands are covered with calluses."*
*etymology:* "pine" √?

## PIS

*This is a substantive. It is antonym of* "lak". *"Lak" is any spot darker in color as compared to the background, and "Pis" is any spot which is lighter in color. Thus* "Dastew pis wode." *"His hand has developed blotches of discolored skin."*
"Pust e dastew lak o pis-e." *"The skin of his hand has dark and whitish spots on it."*
"pisi" = *leprosy, a disease, causing whitish spots on the skin.*
"pisi" = *vitiligo. figuratively,* "pisi" = *poverty, hardship.* "Saxt be pisi oftáde." *"He is in hardship: either has no money or he is having a tough time, with not much reserve (physical or emotional)."*
[*etymology*: pis < paesa-, (Avest) *1- one affected with vitiligo, 2- vitiligo, leprosy, 3- decoration. Picás (Old Indian)(decoration).*]

# PIWI

"piwi" = *"a pussy, a pussy cat"*

"Piwi biyá!" *"Come on, pussy cat!"*

[*etymology*: piwi-,; piw-, *cf* fawo-, *(Avest) small useful tamed animal*.]

# POF

1- *swelling*: "Loppew pof kard." *"His cheek swelled up."* "Zanbur zad, dastew pof kard." *"A wasp stung him, his hand swelled up."* "Nun pof kard." *"The bread puffed up."*

2- *figuratively*: "pof kardan": *to put on airs, to take pride in...* "Xeyli (be xodet) pof nakon, bádet dar mire!" *"Don't put on airs! You'll be deflated."*

[*etymology: See and cf* papu, pok, puc, pofyuz.]

# POFYUZ

*This is a substantive. It is a pejorative term. "Pofyuz" is used when referring to a man (not a woman), who is worthless and good-for-nothing. Sometimes a meaning of disgraced or dishonored is also understood from this word. "Martike ye pofyuz, hey doruq mige." "The "despicable" man, constantly lies."*

[*etymology*: √?: ? pofyuz = pof-yuz: pof *cf*. puk, puc, pok, pof; yuz *cf*. युध् *yudh (Sanskrit) to fight, struggle, contend with, cf*. "razm-yuz" *"one who is a fighter, who contends with...."*; "palang-yuz" *"one who fights with a leopard."* "dar-yuz" *and* "cáh-yuz". *Also compare with* "pof-yuz"]

# POK

"Pok" *is a noun. Almost always used as* "pok zadan": *to puff at.* "pok" = *a puff.* "Do se tá pok be qelyunew zad o goft...." *"He gave a few puffs at his waterpipe and said...."*

[*etymology and semantic reconstruction: cf*. pap-u, puw, puk, puc, pof. *Indo-European base* "bu," bhu-, *to blow out, or up, swell, inflate. Also cf English words: pod, bud, pocket, poke, pock, pox. Also cf* पुट: *putáh (Sanskrit): 1- a hollow space, cavity, 2- a vessel made of leaves, 3- any shallow receptacle, 4- the pod or capsule, 5- a sheath, cover(ing):* पुत: *putah; putáhan imitative word expressive of hard breathing or blowing*.]

## POKIDAN

"pokidan" = *to burst open.* "Delam az qam pokid." *"My heart burst with grief."*
[*etymology and semantic reconstruction: see* "pok"]

## POX

*This word is commonly thought to mean "feces, ordure, excrement", however it is never used in this sense. It is almost always used when referring to people who are incompetent and who cannot exert any influence. Thus it is almost always used "figuratively", and never in the sense of "feces, stools".*
"Goft káret o dorost mikonam." *"He said, "I will fix your job for you (do not worry)"* "Goftam: na bábá poxi nist, kári azaw bar nemiyád." *"I retorted: "no! come on! He is no big shot, he cannot effect anything."*
[*etymology:* √ ?; *1- cf* "pox": pix *(pus, grime);* pix-ál *(feces, excrement, pus, dirt, grime);* pus, pusidan *(to putrefy); cf* पूति *puti (Sanskrit) putrid, stinking* पुय् *puy (Sanskrit) to putrefy;* पूति:: *putih: filth, pus, matter. Cf* pox *(Turkish)(feces, excrement)*]

## POZ

"Poz e áli, jib e xáli," *"He looks dandy, but he has nothing in his pockets."*
"Pozew áli-ye." *"His appearance is excellent."* *"He is well-dressed."*
"Poz nade." *"Don't brag!"* *"don't show off!"*
"Hey poz miyámad, xitew kardam." *"He bragged a lot, I rebuked him!"*
*etymology: ? from pose (French)*

## PUC

*This is a substantive. It is applied to thoughts, ideas, plans which are devoid of meaning, sense and orientation. Also lottery tickets, which are not winner, can be called* "puc".
"Harfáw hame puc-e." *"His talks are all nonsense."*
"Bilitew puc dar umad." *"His lottery ticket is not winner."*
*etymology: Cf* "pok", "puk".

## PUK

1- *empty: any fruit kernel, nut or pod, without a seed or substance in it.* "In gerdu puk-e." *"This walnut has no pulp."*

2- *figuratively*: "kalle puk!" *"You knuckle head!, you idiot!"* *"You, whose skull is devoid of brain."*

3- *fragile*, "Ostoxunáw puk wode." *"His bones are rarefied, or osteoporotic."*
*etymology: See* "puc", pok".

# PUW

"puw" *fluffed, fluffy;* "puw dádan" = *to fluff*

"Muháw o puw dád." *"She blew her hair until they were loose and fluffy."*

"Bálew o puw dád." *"She fluffed the pillow."* *"She shook or patted it until it became feathery and fluffy."*
*etymology: See* "pok".

# PUZ

"Puz" *is "muzzle" or the anterior part of the head of animals such as cats, dogs, donkeys. "Puz" consists of the nose, the mouth, the chin, the lips, the circumoral area and a small area of the cheeks adjacent to the lips.*

"Puzew o kard tu áb." *"He stuck his muzzle into the water."*

"Puzaw deráz-e." *"Its muzzle is long."*
*etymology:* √?

# Q

## QALANDAR

"Qalandar" *is a man who is magnanimous and is not bound by material needs. A "qalandar" engages in activities worthy of a man. One truly enlightened, and detached from worldly needs and attachments.*

[*etymology*: qalandar = qalan-dar ≡ karan-dar: *cf.* कर kara (Sanskrit), करा kará *who or what does, makes or causes.* "dar" *cf dharma (Sanskrit)* = *duty. Thus "one who engages in duties (of life)".*] [*cf* kalán-tar *(elder; sheriff). If this is correct, then the root is different.*]

## QALT

"qalt" = *rolling;"* "qaltidan" = "qalt zadan" *to roll (vi);* "qalt xordan" = *to roll over (vi).* "Qalt" *is mostly used for animate beings whereas* "qel" *is mostly used for inanimate objects. see* "qel".
"Cerá xarqalt mizani?" *"Why you are rolling (in bed, etc)?"* [ xar: *big, not related to donkey*]
"Qalt zad oftád tu jub." *"He rolled over (while sleeping) and fell into the creek."*
[*etymology*: qalt < *vrit (Sanskrit): See* "qel", "qer".]

## QAMBÁD

"Qambád" *is a goiter.* "Zanew qambád darávorde." *"His wife has developed a goiter."*
[*etymology*: qambád = qam-bád: qam = *grief, sorrow:* bád: *swelling* < váta *(Avest) wind.* "Qambád" *a swelling due to grief and sorrow.*]

## QAMBIL

qoum o qambil, qambile;
*A depreciative term when referring to someone's relatives, and folks.*
"Qoum o qambilewam vardáwte ávorde." *"He has brought his folks with himself."*
[*etymology*: qoum *(Arabic), a people, and* "qabile" *(Arabic) a tribe. pejoratively persified* qoum قوم *and* qabile قبیله *from Arabic.*]

## QANJ

*Only the modern meaning in common use is given here.* "Qanj" *is a noun. It is always used in the following form:* "Qanj zadan, del e kasi":
"Delew qanj mizad." *"He is so happy and rejoicing something very pleasant."*
"Delam qanj mizane." *"I am very happy and I rejoice it."*
"Dar dánewkade ye pezewki pazirofte wode, delew qanj mizane." *"He is admitted to the medical school. He is very happy and rejoices it very much."*
[*etymology*: qanj: *cf* "xanj" *and* "xanje": *the sound emitted at the time of climax during sexual intercourse. cf* कंजन *kanjana: the god of love.*]

## QAZAN-QURTAKI

*This is an adjective. It is pejorative and is used in a depreciating manner.* "Qazanqurtaki" *is used in reference to a person who is vainly boastful but of no real achievement. Thus* "Hey miyád injá, qiyáfehá ye qazanqurtaki migire!" *(He comes here frequently and he puts on an air of false victory or importance!)*
[*etymology and semantic reconstruction*: qazan; qaz-an; -an *is a suffix denoting a place. Thus:* -an *and* –án, Káw-án, Semn-án, Kerm-án. "-an" *in* "qazan" *equivalent* "-án" *(a patronymic suffix).* Qaz-, = qáz: *compare with* kawa-, *(Avest)*; xazar *(Caspian Sea)* kawa-, = *a big cut; gulf; sinus)-; cf* Vouru-kawa *(Caspian sea; A sea with wide* (vouru) *gulfs and sinuses* (kawa). *From the same root we derive:* Qazvin *(name of a town);* Caspian *(English);* Kasvin, Kawvin, *(Old names for Qazvin) and* kaw *(armpit). cf* Qázán *(name of a town; a place related to a gulf). Thus* "Qázánwáh *(The ruler of* "qázán. *Thus* "qazan" *is synonymous with* "qázán", *name of a place or town related to a gulf.*
qurt-ak-i; -i *is a suffix denoting relationship.*
-ak *is a diminutive suffix*
qurt = gord *(a hero)*
*Thus* "qazan-qurtaki" *is* "like a hero of Qázán". *"the hero of a gulf-town or harbor-town".*]

## QÁC

"Qác" *is a noun. It means a* "slice", *specially of fruits such as watermelon, melon, honeydew etc.* "Ye qác be man bede." *"Give me a slice".* "Henduna ro qác kon!" *"Slice the watermelon!"* [*cf* kawa- *(Avest) and* qazan-qurtaki]
*etymology*: qác = qáw, qáj *(<Turkish)* = 1-crack, 2- slice. *(BQM p.2607)* [!?]

## QÁCÁQ

*This is a substantive . It means, smuggle, or smuggling, smuggled.*
"In tanbáku qácáq-e." *"This is a contraband tobacco."*
"Barádarew qácáq mikone." *"His brother smuggles things."*
*etymology*: qácáq *(Turkish): sleight of hand.*

## QÁL

*I know of three combinations with this word, which is never used alone:*
1- "qál gozáwtan": "Má ro qál gozowt." *"He made us wait and disappeared on us."*
*"He left us behind, without letting us know of his intentions."*
2- "qál mándan": "qál mund, havápeymá raft." *"He was left behind, the airplane left, without him."*
3- "Qál e cizi rá kandan": "Qál e qaziy ya ro kand." *"He finished with that matter."*
*etymology*: < ?? qál غال *(Arabic): (1- to take a thing unexpectedly. 2- to cause something to perish (waterless land): 3- to assassinate, 4- to intoxicate someone (with wine).)*

## QÁLTÁQ

*This is a substantive. Meaning: a cheat, swindler. This word can be used as an adjective or noun. Thus: "Xeyli qáltáq-e." (He is a big cheater.)*
"Pesare ye qáltáq pul e doxtara ro dozdid o dar-raft." *(The rogue stole the girl's money and made off with it.) This is a pejorative term.*
[*etymology and semantic reconstruction: qált-áq: "-áq" may be a suffix equivalent of -ak; -a; -ah; and -ax or it may be considered as equivalent of "axv'" such as that found in words as "farrox", "duzax", "barzax". qáh, ≡ harz, harz+axv, cf. "qaltban"*
qált: *Cf"qal" (Pashtu language)(a thief; burglar); cf* छलिन् *chálin (Sanskrit)(a cheat; swindler; rogue);* छल:: *cháláh;* छलं *chálán (Sanskrit)(fraud; trick; deceit; deception; roguery; knavery). Also cf "wárlátán" (charlatan; a rogue; cheat); and "qor zadan")]*

## QÁPPIDAN

"qáppidan" = *to snatch.* "Sag guwt o tu havá qáppid." *"The dog snatched the meat in the air."* "Az dastam qápid." *"He grabbed it from my hand."*
*etymology*:? < qápmáq *(Turkish) to steal, to rob. (BQM p.2606)*

## QÁQ

1- "Qáq" *is an adjective. It denotes something "bony dry". "Kunew qáq-e."* "*His rear end is lean, fatless and bony." "To ke qáqe qáq-i." "You are a bag of bones!" "Nun e qáq." "Dry bread and nothing else." "Angowtew o az bas mikide qáq wode." "His finger is bony dry, because he's sucked on it so much."*

2- *"To qáq-i un dim-e." "(dar qáb bázi); In a Persian gambling game: you must play last, he must play first." (see* "dim")

[*etymology:* "qáq" *cf:* कक्खटी *kákháti (Sanskrit): solid, hard,* "qáq" *(Arabic loanword?): a skinny lanky man.*]

## QÁQÁ

*This is a noun. It is used when talking to infants (not even children). It means, "sweets", "candy". "Bebin nini qáqá mixore." "See (how) the baby eats sweets."*

*etymology:* √? [*cf* kák *a sort of cake*]

## QÁRÁWMIW

*This word means "a mess", "a disorderly mixture of some incongruous things or persons". Thus "In kár xeyli qáráwmiw-e." "This work is a big mess."*

[*etymology:* qara, qárá, gerán, kalán, *all derived from the same root meaning "big", "colossal".* "miw", "mix", -ámiz, (mix). *Thus: a big mixture.* "-w-" *between* "qárá" *and* "miw" *most probably of Turkish origin.* ]

## QÁTI

"qáti" = *mixed, mingled.* "qáti-páti", *badly mixed or confused.*

"Mást o bá áb qáti kon!". *"Mix the yogurt with water."*

"Hama ro qáti páti kard." *"He mixed up everything. He made a big mess."*

*etymology:* "qáti" *qátmak, qátmaq (Turkish) = mixed (BQM p.2607)*

## QEL, QELQEL, QELQELI

"qel xordan," "Qel xord raft tu suláx." *"It rolled and dropped into the hole."*

"qel zadan": "Qel (qel) zad tu caman." *"He rolled (over, and over) on the lawn."*

"qelqeli": "Kufte qelqeli xordim." *"We ate meat balls."* Doxtare ye (kufte) qelqeli" *"The plump (rotund) girl."*

[*etymology:* qel < √ vrit *(Sanskrit): to roll.*

103

Semantic reconstruction: *cf* qel; qer; gerd; gawtan; vardane, vawtan, vawt, qalt, gardidan.]

## QELEQ
*This word is synonymous with "lemm" in most instances.*
*"Qeleq e in máwin hanuz dastam nayumade." "I have not yet got the feel of this machine (or car)."*
*But in the following instance not synonymous with "lemm".*
*"Ádam e bad-qeleqi-ye." "He is a moody man and in dealing with him one must know how to approach him."*
*etymology:* √? *cf* kalak

## QELQEL, QELQELI
*See "qel".*

## QER
*"Qer" is a noun. It means a danceful movement. "qer umadan": "qer nayá!"*
*"1- Don't make a danceful movement.!" "2- Get to the work. Stop fooling around. Get to the gist of the matter." "3- Emruz havá hey qer miyád."*
*"Today the weather is very unstable." "qer dádan": "De qer nade." "1- Stop making danceful movements. 2- No figurative meaning in contrast to "qer umadan."*
[*etymology: See "qel"* < *vrit* वृत, *varnayatih* वर्नयति: *to turn, roll on, revolve.*]

## QEREWMÁL
*"Qerewmál" is a substantive. It refers to a girl or a woman who is quarrelsome, and wants to have things her own way primarily by screaming and loud quarreling.*
*"Doxtare ye qerewmál, enqad jiq zad ke guwam kar wod." "The shrew girl, "cried" me to deafness."*
[*etymology:* qerew-mál:
qerew *cf.* xoruw, xorus, qerqi, kaláq, kark, xrustan < क्रुश् *kruw (Sanskrit)(to cry; lament; 2- to cry out; yell; scream 3- to call out);* क्रोश: *krowáh (Sanskrit)(a cry; yell; shout; scream; noise)*
-mál? mar *(Avest);* wmar-, *(Avest); cf* womordan; már; ámár; mar; morur; mra-ow, mru *(Avest)(to say; utter)]*

## QERMEQUZI

"Qermequzi minevise!" *"He scribbles." "His handwriting is like cat-scratch." "qermequzi" = very crooked.*

[*etymology*: qermequzi = qerm-e-quzi: qerm = kerm, कृमि *krimi (Sanskrit) = a worm; quzi-quz-i; quz = kuź, guź; Thus "qermequzi = a crooked, or humped worm. The poor hand-writing is likened to crooked, humped worms.*
quz < kuź *cf* आकुंच् *ákunc: to crook, to curve, bend, contract, heap;* आकुंचित *ákuncitá: crooked, curved, bent, contracted, heaped.*]

## QENÁS

*This is a substantive. It is applied to anything which is not symmetrical in shape.*
"In zamin qenáse." *"This lot of land is not of a regular geometric shape."*
"In dáman qenáse." *"This skirt is irregular or asymmetric in shape."*
*etymology*: √?

## QERQEWE

See "qewqere".

## QERTI

*This is a substantive. It is referred to an adolescent boy or young man or woman (not to children or elderly people). It denotes somebody who is too obsessed with his or her appearance. One who dresses dandy, and leads a leisurely life, and fools around with opposite sex. One who is not hard-working, and does not pursue character building.*
"Pesare ye qerti hanuz kelás e hawtom-e." *"The "qerti" lad is still in the 8th grade (he has flunked many times.)"*
*etymology: See "qer".*

## QESER

*This is used only as* "qeser darraftan." *"To save one's skin," "to escape unharmed." "Yáru xub qeser darraft." "The guy escaped unharmed." "Xub qeser dar raftiyá!" "You know, you escaped unharmed very nicely!"*
*etymology*: < ? qeser *(Arabic): Shortness*
        < ? قسر *(Arabic): to make someone work by force. forced labor [?!]*

## QEWQERE, QERQEWE, XARXAWE

"Qewqere" *is referred to any loud fussing and disputing.* "Umad azam pul begire. Goftam nadáram, nemiduni ce qewqereyi be pá kard." *"He came to get some money. I told him, that I had none. You can't imagine what a (noisy) fuss he made."*

[*etymology: cf* कर्कश: *karkawáh: (callous, harsh, cruel, merciless, (words, conduct, etc.) - violent; strong; excessive; ill-conducted) unchaste.*]

## QEYQÁJ

*This word is usually used as an adverb, meaning "in a very crooked manner". Thus* "Qeyqáj mirune!" *(He drives in a crooked manner.)* "Cerá qeyqáj ráh miri?" *(Why do you walk zigzag?).*

[*etymology*: qeyqáj = kaj-kaj, *(zigzag)*]

## QIN = KUN

"Qin" *is a noun. It is synonymous with* "kun" = *the ass, anus.*
"Boro dar e qinet o (kunet o) bezár." *(abusive.): "Go and stop up your ass-hole!" (Do not interfere with my business. Do not put your nose into my business!"*

*etymology: § kun*

## QOBBE, QOPPE

"Qobbe" *is a noun. Any small object similar to a mound or hillock is called a* "qobbe". *Thus, a knob, boss or cupola.*
"Qoppehá ye morabbá ru ye nun." *"Small mounds of jam on the bread."*
"Timsár ru duwew se tá qoppe dáre, do tá setáre." *"The general has three knobs and two stars on his shoulder-piece."*

[*etymology*: qobbe = qoppe = koppe: kop-(p)-e: kop *cf* kuh *(mountain):* kaofa-, *(Avest),* kaufa *(Old Persian).*]

## QOL

1- "Áb qol(qol) mizane." *"The water is boiling (and emitting bubbles)".*
2- "Biyá ye qol do qol bázi konim." *"Come on, let's play"* "ye qol do qol". *"(a game of children, using 5 small pebbles.)"*
"Do qolu záyid." *"She gave birth to twins."* "Se qolu záyid." *"She gave birth to a triplet."*

"Ye qolew o to vardár, do qolew o bede man." *"You take one piece, and I take two pieces."*
[*etymology*: 1- qol, *bubbling, boiling: cf* garm, gorm, hor, horm, gor. 2- qol: *probably a contracted form of* "jumul-u: *(Shirázi dialect) = twin cf gemini, geminus (Latin) = twin, gemel (English) either of two units.*]

## QOLCOMÁQ
*This is a substantive. It is commonly applied to men (sometimes women) who try to bully others.* "Nemiduni ce qolcomáqi-ye!" *"You can't imagine what a bully he is.!"*
[*etymology and semantic reconstruction*: qol-comáq:
qol-, *prefix, compare with* "qoldor". "qol" *(big; thick; heavy; coarse)*
See "kalfatár" *and* "koloft".
"comáq" *(a mace, a club)(Turkish). Thus* "qolcomáq" *literally one with a heavy club/mace.*

## QOLDOR
*This is a substantive. It is used almost synonymous with* "qolcomáq".
"Cerá qoldor-bázi darmiyári?" *(Why you bully people?)*
"Bábá xeyli qoldor-e!" *(That guy is a big bully!)*
[*etymology and semantic reconstruction*:
qol-, *From the same root are derived* "gerán", "qolcomáq", "qolve", "quc" "qul", "qor", "xar-," *(as in* xarpul; xarzur); "kal-án *(big, great); also see* "qolcomáq" *and* "karfatár".
*Cf* गुरू *guru; gurvi (Sansk)(heavy; weighty);* गरियस् *gariyas (1- heavy; weighty 2- great; large 3- important; great 4- arduous; difficult to bear etc)*
dor: d → j.. → c *thus*: dor = cor *(penis)*(dor = penis also noted in dialects.)
*Thus* "qoldor" *(= kir koloft)(one who has a thick dick, thus figuratively "a bully")*]

## QOLONBE
*This is a substantive. It means a protuberance, a bulge.*
"Muw o zir e cárqad qolombe karde." *"She has made a ball of her hair under the scarf and that ball makes a bulge on her scarf."*
"Ye báre ewqew qolonbe wod!" *"(figuratively): All of a sudden he wanted to express his love to...."*
*etymology: See* áblambu.

## QOLOP

1- "Ye qolop boxor." *"Take a mouthful (only of liquids.)"*

2- "Qolop qolop wiwa ro sar kewid." *"He drank up all (the bottle), in big gulps."*

3- "Áb az wiwe qolop qolop mirize birun." *"The water pours out of the bottle, making a gurgling sound."*

4- "Cewmáw qolop zad birun." *"His eyes bulged out or came out of their orbits."*

*etymology: Cf* qort, qurt, hort.

## QOLVE

"qolve" *is a noun, meaning a kidney, usually when referring to it as a food.*
"Del o qolve kabáb xordim." *"We ate a kabob of heart and kidney." " we ate grilled heart and kidney."*

"qolve sang": *a rock, round and as big as a kidney.* "Ráh por e qolve-sang bud." *"The road was strewn with rocks."*

"Del dáde qolve gerefte." *"She was so engrossed in talking (with somebody)"*
[qol-ve, kol-ye, *cf* kalfatár, < qol-, ger-,]

## QOMBOL

"Qombol" *is a substantive.  It is synonymous with* "qolombe."
"Kunew o qombol karde." *"She makes her buttocks bulge."*
*etymology*: qombol: *cf* "qolombe", *and* "gombad"

## QOMPOZ

*This is a noun, almost always used with* "dar kardan", *thus* "qompoz dar kardan", *means* "to show off, to brag about, to act ostentatiously."
"Ráh mire o qompoz dar mikone." *"He constantly brags about (his deeds)."*
"Bas kon!  Qompoz dar nakon!" *"Stop your showing off or bragging!"*
*etymology*: qompoz = qom-poz, qom?; poz , *see* "poz"

## QOND (ZADAN)

*(to squat)*
"Gorbehe ru táqce qond zade." *"The cat is squatting on the shelf."*
*etymology and semantic reconstruction*: gundak *(Pahlavi)*, gund *(Armenian)*, gndak *(Armenian) = a ball, a sphere, (BQM p.1843).*

[*semantic reconstruction: basic concept: any ball-shaped thing: cf* qondáq, qonce, qond, condak, combátme; gonde, gond *(a testic)*]

## QONDÁQ

"Qondáq" *is a "swaddling cloth", "a papoose";* "qondáq kardan" *"to swaddle", "to put in a papoose".*

"Bacca ro qondáq kon!" *"Swaddle the baby."*

"Qondáqew o báz kon." *"Undo her (his) papoose."*

"Qondáq" *also means the "butt of a rifle."* "Zad bá qondáq e tofang, dar o wikund." *"He broke the door by hitting it with the butt of his rifle."*

[*etymology: and semantic reconstruction: basic concept, any round, ball-like object. See* "qond".]

## QOR

1- "qor zadan" "qorqor zadan": *to grumble.*

2- "Doxtari yá zani rá qor zadan": *"to deceive a girl or a woman":* "Doxtar e hamsáya ro qor zad." *"He deceived his neighbor's daughter."*

3- "Qor wodan": "Un sang o var nadár qor miwi." *"Don't lift that rock, you'll get a hernia (a rupture)."*

"Zad máwinam o qor kard." *"He collided with (bumped into) my car and my car (the body of my car) was dented."*

[*etymology: 1- "qor" = grumbling, is of onomatopoeic origin.*

2- qor zadan: *= to deceive:* √ ?

3- "qor wodan": *to develop a swelling or a bump, to become dented, depressed or sunken.* √? <? xvahl, xal, xol.]

"qorzadan" *(vt)* "kasi rá qor zadan" *(to deceive, to bring someone under one's thumb or influence)*

"Pesare doxtara ro qor zad." *(The young man deceived the girl and made love with her.)*

"Doxtare pesara ro qor zad." *(The girl deceived the boy and eventually made him marry her.)*

"Qorew zadand" *(They deceived him and brought him under their control.)*

[*etymology: qor-, compare with* "qáltáq", *also cf qál (Pashtu) (thief)*]

## QORÁZE

*This is a substantive. It is used to describe machines, gadgets, devices etc, which are old, decrepit, and not functioning efficiently, or breaking down repeatedly.*
"Saváre docarxe ye qorázaw wod raft, ammá miyun e ráh pancar wod." *"He rode his "junk"-bike and left, but he had a flat (tire) on the road."*
*etymology: "qoráze" derived from the "Arabic" word: "qoráza", chips, broken pieces.*

## QOROMSÁQ

"Qoromsáq" *is a substantive. It is a pejorative term. It means a man (not a woman) who is a cuckold. A man who tolerates the infidelity of his wife.*
"Hey migan qorom qorom tá be qoromsáq ádat kone." *"One can tolerate disgrace, by being pulled into it in a gradual fashion."*
"Qoromsáq zanew o nemibine, az doxtar e má eyb migire!" *"The cuckold is blind on his wife, but he finds fault with our daughter."*

## QORT, QORT-QORT

"qort" = *drinking rapidly and noisily.*
"qort(qort) xordan" = *to drink noisily and rapidly.*
"Ye qort boxor!" *"Take or drink a gulp of it!"*
[*etymology: cf* "qurt" *to swallow, swallowing*
"Qort" *is most probably of onomatopoeic origin. However the phonetic structure of the word also lends itself easily to:* xordan = xvordan. *To eat, to swallow. Also cf* xor, xord, xordan, hort, qurt, qort, sur (xatne-surán).]

## QOZ

*This is a substantive. It is applied to individuals who are ugly, specifically people of low stature, with crooked limbs, back and nose.*
"Bábá be rixt e qozew negáh nemikone, kot o walvár e Ivsanlorán mixád."
*"The unshapely guy not considering his shape, wants to have an Ives St Laurant suit!"*
[*etymology:* qoz, = kuź, *see* "qermequzi" *and* "quz".]

## QOZMIT

"Qozmit" *is a substantive. It is applied to anything or any individual of crooked shape and poor value.*

"Ye máwin e qozmit dáre, xeyli behew mináze." *"He takes pride in his car, which is a junk."*

"Doxtare xeyli qozmit-e." *"That girl is awfully unshapely."*

[*etymology*: qozmit = qoz-mit: qoz *cf* kaź *(crooked)*, kuź, guź, quz, *see* "quz" *and* "qormequzi".

-mit, -mit, *(suffix) cf* -mat: *eg.* hurmat, hur-mat, (hur = xor = *the sun*), *and* -mat *(suffix)*(Abdul Rahmáne Emádi, Irán Náme).]

## QULTAWAN

*This is a substantive. It means "gigantic", "having the form of a giant."*

"Martike ye qultawan dar o váz kard o umad tu." *"The giant (corpulent) man opened the door and came inside."*

[*etymology*: qultawan = qul-taw-an: qul *(a giant)*; taw ≡ táw, táwidan *(Pahlavi), to form, shape, hew;* √* taw *(Avest) to cut, to shape,* táwitan *(Pahlavi),* taw *(Soghdian) to cut (BQM p.480).*]

## QURT (DÁDAN)

*to swallow. also see* "qort"

"Bacce sekka ro qurt dád." *"The child swallowed the coin."*

"Har ce qurt midam páyin nemire." *"The more I swallow, it won't go down."*

*etymology: See* "qort".

## QUZ

"Quz" *is a hump.* "Powtew quz dáre." *"He is hump-backed."* "damáqew quz dáre." *"He has an aquiline nose."* "Cerá quz kardi?" *"Why are you stooping?" "Why are you squatting?"* "Sar e quz oftáde." *"He's become stubborn."*

[*etymology*: quz = guź, kuź, guź *(convex)*.]

# R

**RADD**

"Radd e…rá gereftan" *to track or trace something or somebody…*
"Raddew o gereft tá tu ye jangal peydáw kard." *"He traced him and found him in the woods."*
[*etymology*: rad. *cf* रथ्या *ráthyá (Sanskrit): a road, a highway.*]

**RAJ**

"Raj" *is a "row", "a line".*
"Ye raj benevis, ye raj nanevis." *"Write every other line. Write on one line, and leave one line blank."*
"Raj e bálá." *"The upper row or line."*
"Mawqew o raj mizane." *"(The pupil) writes in "raj's": "Raj zadan": is a specific term for writing a single word from top of the page to the bottom, rather than writing one full sentence and then rewriting the whole thing on the second and third lines consecutively."*
[*etymology: rag: रच् rác, रचयति racayáti.*

*1- to arrange, prepare, plan 2- to make, form, effect 3- to write, compose, put together as a work 4- to place in or upon, fix on.*
raj-ist-ak *(Pahlavi) (correct, true, right, just, most honest) (BF p.474), -ist, (superlative adjective-forming suffix), -ak (suffix); raj: cf* रच् *rác (vide supra).]*

**RAMAQ**

"Ramaq" *means "strength, stamina".*
"Ramaq nadáre." = "Biramaq-e." *He is weak/listless (physically and/ or mentally). "He has no stamina."*
"Xeyli azaw kár kewidan, dige ramaq nadáre." *"He has been made to work very hard." "He is exhausted."*
"In cáyi ke ramaq nadáre." *"This tea has no strength (is very weak)."*
[*etymology*: ramaq =? ram-aq: ram *cf* राम *rámá 1- pleasing, delightful, rejoicing, 2- lovely, beautiful, charming 3- white, 4- black; -aq = -ax, cf* axv: *see "damaq."]*

## REND

*a crook.*

"rend": *Modern meaning of this substantive is given below.*

*"Rend" is used to refer to any individual who shrewdly uses the circumstances to cheat people and have things to his benefit.*

"Xeyli rendi, man o mindázi tu hacal, xodet darmiri?" *"You are very smart, you get me involved, and you yourself run away?"*

"Xeyli marde rend-e!" *"He is a big cheat." "He is a crook."*

*The old meaning of this word is someone who maintains a poor appearance however inwardly he is an honest and honorable man. Thus the modern concept of deceitfulness."*

*etymology:* √?

## RIQ = RIX

riq: *1- diarrhea, 2- loose watery stool.*

"Riq zade!" = *1- He has diarrhea. 2- figuratively: He is terrified as a consequence of being confronted with a difficult task.*

"Pesare ye riqu, mixád sang e sad kiluyi bezane." *"The puny boy, wants to lift a 100-kilo weight."*

"Riqew dar umad." *"1- It was squashed, so its juice came out." "2- He/she is exhausted."*

[*etymology and semantic reconstruction:* riq < √ *ri (Sanskrit) to pour out, to evacuate. "raec", (Avest); to pour out. Cf* ridan, rixtan, liz, lajan, luwan, gorixtan. *"ridan" and "rixtan" both closely related.*]

## RIQMÁSSI

*This word refers to individuals who are awfully thin, skinny and lean. It is pejorative and usually signifies leanness due to illness especially diarrhea.*

"Riqmássi umade bá man kowti begire!" *"The bag of bones, wants to wrestle with me."*

[*etymology: Although this word is taken to be equivalent of* "rewkimási" *in some formal books (Amsál o Hekam e Dehkhoda). I believe that its slang version i.e.* "riqmássi" *is more correct. thus:* riqmássi = riq-máss-i: Riq, *see* "riq; mass = mast? *mastu (Sanskrit)* मस्तु = sour cream, whey, (yoghurt) and* "mássidan" *to clot, to become solid as fat exposed to cold. cf mecum (Armenian)(sour milk), macanim (Armenian)(to clot) (BQM p.429),* riqmássi:

*literally somebody who had diarrhea.*]

## RISE

"Rise" *is a noun. Most of the time it is used as:* "rise raftan". "Rise" *is a breath-holding spell noted primarily in children.*
"Bacce rise raft, áb behew zadim, hálew já umad." *"The child had a breath-holding spell, we sprinkled water on him, and he came back to himself."*
[*etymology:* √? rise = ris-e? *close to* "risidan", "rewtan" *(to spin,)? A series of spells, similar to a* "rise" *or a spun filament, a chain phenomenon, a chain reaction.*]

## RIX

*See* "riq"

## ROSS

*This is a noun, always used with* "kewidan", *thus* "Ross e cizi yá kasi rá kewidan", *means* "to exhaust something or someone of juice or strength."
"Ross e má ro kewid." *"He made us work hard and exhausted us."*
"Ross e bátri ro kewid." *"It really drew the juice out of the battery."*
*etymology:* √?

# S

## SALITE

*This is a substantive.  It is referred only to girls or women.  It denoted a woman who is belligerent and who has a shrill cry.  She would cause a scandal, if bothered.  A shrew.*

"Doxtare ye salite áberum o bord."  *"The shrew, scandalized (disgraced) me."*
*etymology:* √? < *Arabic.*

## SAMBAL

"Sambal kardan" *means "to bungle."*

"Ámad divár o rang kone, natunest, sambalew kard."  *"He wanted to paint the wall, he couldn't do (a good job) it, he bungled it."*

"Natunest jáváb e man o bede, ye juri sambal kard."  *"He could not answer my question, thus he covered the topic perfunctorily."*

[*etymology:* sambal = sam-bal: sam-, = ham-, < *sámá (Sanskrit): together.*  bal ≡ bar ≡ var? < भृ *bhri: to carry, take.  Cf.* संभृ *sámbhri: 1- to collect, hoard, place or bring together, 2- to make ready, prepare.*]

## SAQQ

*This word means the hard (and? soft) palate.  It is commonly used as:*
"Saqqam suxt."  *"(I drank or ate something hot), I burned my (hard) palate."*
"Saqqew siyás."  *"His (hard) palate is black."  Whatever bad things he says or predicts, come to pass."*
*etymology: literally:* saqq? = saqf, *the ceiling.*  saq (Borujerdi, Kermánwáhi, Aráki)*(1- the ceiling, 2- the hard palate.)* (FM p.1886) (BQM p.1141).

## SÁNJU

*This is a noun.  It means "a chest cold", "pleuritis", or probably "pneumonia".  "Sánju", is associated with fever, cough and pain in the chest wall or flanks.*

"Loxt naro birun sánju mikoni."  *"Don't go out bare, you'll catch a chest cold."*

"Tu barfá raft tu houz, sánju kard."  *"He took a bath in the pond, in (deep) snow, he developed a chest cold."*

[*etymology*: sánju = sán-ju: sán ≡ sem, zem: √ हिम *himá (Sanskrit) cold. Cf* Himá-láyá, zemestán, zám-harir, zám-in, *and* "ju" √?]

## SEMEJ

*This is a substantive. It refers to an individual who is relentlessly insistent, and perseverant in his quest.*
"Mes e gedáhá ye Sámere semej-e." *"He is like the beggars of* "samara"; *he is relentless, and won't give up, until he gets what he wants."*
*etymology*: semej: ? < *Arabic* "samoj", *to be ugly:* "samájat": *ugliness, rudeness, roughness. [?!!]*

## SENDE

"Sende" *is a formed, hard (or dry) stool.; turd*
"Sag e sende endáxt/kard." *"The dog defecated (and dropped or made a hard stool.)"*
*Pejoratively it is applied to people of no worth.*
"Sende engár az damáq e fil oftáde." *"The despicable man, thinks very high of himself."*
*etymology:* √?

## SERTEQ, SERTEX

"Serteq" *is a substantive. It is applied to an individual of hot temper who in order to have things her way, would cause lots of noise and disturbance. It is mostly used for females.*
"Doxtare ye serteq, vaqti behew goftan pul nist, xewtakew o kewid sarew."
*"The shrew (girl), caused a scandal, when she was told that there was no money (left)."*
*etymology:* √?

## SEY = SI

"sey" = "si" = *for, on the account of.*
"Yeki si xodet vardár, yeki si man." *"Take one for yourself, and one for me."*
"Vásey e ci injá váysádi?" *"What are you standing here for?" (On the account of what?).*
"Bosey e (váse ye) xodet delet besuze." *"Pity yourself! Don't feel pity for others."*

[*etymology*: vásey e = bosey e = be+ sey+ e: *on the account of, for..... for the sake of.* sey = si = vasnád. "vasnád *(Pahlavi) (on the account of, for) (BF p.583)*.]

## SI

*See* "sey".

## SITE-SOMÁQI

*Applied to girls or women who are talkative, outspoken, not shy and usually witty.* "Doxtaráw site-somáqi-yan." *"His daughters are* "sitesomáqi." *"Outspoken and talkative."*
[*etymology*: site = suxte *(burned). also cf* "suta": "Hame suta-delán gerd e ham áyid". suxtan < √ saoc *(Avest),* saoka-, *(to light); Site-somáqi: roasted to dark purple color, as the color of sumac.*]

## SIM

"Sim kewidan": "Dastew zaxm bud, zad be áb, sim kewid. *"He had a sore on his hand, he exposed it to water, it became infected. (Or developed thrombophlebitis, or phlebitis.)"*
[*etymology*: astim, ástim: *(abscess, pus);* simeká (Tabari), simká, simkák (Mázandaráni), sima (Mázandaráni)*(BQM p.128)*]

## SIX = WAQ(Q)

"Six" *synonymous with* "waq(q)" *is a substantive. Anything erect and stiff is called* "six" *or* "waq(q). *Thus:*
"Muháw six wod." *"He had horripilation."* *"His hairs stood on end."*
"Kirew six wod, yá waqq wod." *"He got an erection." "He had a hard on."*
"Six miyun e ráh váysáde jomm nemixore." *"He is standing erect in the middle of the way and does not budge."*
[*etymology*: six <? √ stá *(to be erect),* or <? √ (s)taig *to be pointed or sharp,* stija *(Avest) (BQM p.1104) cf* setix, setiq, tiq, tiz, tiwe.
स्था sthá *(Sanskrit): erect,* स्थापयति sthápáyáti *(Sanskrit). Also cf* sok, zoq, soqolme.]

## SOK

"Sok" *is a noun. It means any object with a sharp or pointed end, used to prod or stimulate. Thus a goad, or a prod. It is mostly used with* "zadan". *Thus* "sok zadan" = *to prod.*

"Hey sok mizane." *"He constantly goads." "He constantly pokes."*
"Sok bezan tu pahluw." *"Prod him in his side." "Give him a poke in the side."*
[*eymology*: sok: *See* six; *cf* six, setiq, waq, zoq, zoq-zoq, soqolme.]

## SOQOLME

1- "Soqolme" *is any roughness or unevenness, much as a bump.* "In taxt ke hamaw six o soqolmas." *"This bed is all of spikes and bumps." (It is uneven and rough, thus uncomfortable.)*

2- "soqolme zadan": *to poke, with something with a rounded or sharp end.* "Bá árenjew behem soqolme zad." *"He poked me in my side with his elbow."* "Six o soqolme zad be xare tá ráh oftád." *"He poked the donkey with spikes and blows, to make it run."*

[*etymology*: soqolme = soq-ol-me; soq ≡ six, *see* six.; -ol = ul; *cf* six-ul = porcupine.]

## SORÁQ

"Soráq e…ámadan": *1- to come to visit with someone; to call on somebody. 2- to come to something.*

"Soráq e…raftan": *1- to go to visit with someone, 2- to go after something.*

"Soráq e…rá gereftan": *to inquire about someone or something, to try to find the whereabouts of someone or something.*

"Pas az sálhá umad soráq e doxtare." *"After many years he came back to that same girl."*

"Gorbehe raft soráq e muwe." *"The cat went after the rat."*

"Ye mardi umade soráq e bábá ro migire." *"A man is here, asking about the whereabouts of the father."*

*etymology:* soráq √?; *cf* ? suráx, suláx.

## SU

"Su" *means "light", "a dim light": It is used in the following fashions:*
"Ceráqi az dur susu mizad." *"A light flickered in the distance."*
"Az dur ye kursuyi dide miwod." *"A dim light was seen in the distance."*

"Cewmáw su nadáre." *"His eyes have no light (his vision is dim)."*
"Ti xáxura susu fadáyi?" *(Gilaki dialect) "You showed off your....to your sister, in order to make her envy you (?)."*
[*etymology*: su < saoc-, (Avest); saocayáhi *(to light).* átare-saoka (Avest) *flame of fire.* saocant (Avest) = *burnt. (BQM p.1183)*]

## SUGURME

"Sugurme" *is a noun. It means eyebrows and mid-forehead contracted into a frowning state.*
"Sugurmat o vákon!" *"Don't frown!" (Open the knot on your eyebrows.)*
"Cerá abruhát o sugurme kardi?" *"Why are you frowning?"*
*etymology:* √?

# T

## TABAQ

"tabaq zadan"

"tabaq": *female external genitalia.* "Tabaq zadan" *means self-abuse by girls or women. Stimulation of the external genitalia by rubbing with the hand or against hard objects in order to obtain sexual gratification.*

"Dar gozawte gomán mikardand, tabaq zadan o jalq zadan máye ye bimári miwe." *"It was thought that masturbation in females and males causes disease."*

tabaq, *cf* tabang *(a tray), also*: tapang, tabangu. *(BQM p.1025).*

*etymology:* √?

## TALAKE

"Talake" *means extorting money from somebody.*

"Táksici ye xeyli azaw talake kard." *"The cab-driver ripped him off."*

"Carxsáze  sar e kuce, ahl e talaka-s." *"The bike-shop keeper at the corner is a rip-off."*

[*etymology*: talake = tal-ak-e; -e, = -ak *(suffix);*

*cf* talak: tale, tala, *a trap. thus*: "talake": *like a trap.*

*Also cf* talak: *trap, treppe (German)(stair, step); dravati (Sanskrit)(he runs.)(?)*]

## TALAMBÁR

"Talambár" *is amassing, collecting or a collection, a heap.*

"Talambár kardan", *is to amass, collect, to heap up.*

"Hame ye gandomá ro talambár kardan." *"They heaped up the wheat."*

[*etymology*: talambár = tal-ambár: tal = *a mound, hillock;* ambár *(to store, stow away),* am-, = an-, = ham-,, bár-, pára, < √ par, por *(BQM p.163)*]

## TAMARGIDAN

*See* "betamarg".

## TAQÁS

"Taqásew o pas midi!" *"You'll pay for it!"*

"Taqásew o migiram!" *"I'll take revenge upon you!"* *"I'll make you pay for it!"*

"In kár bi taqás nemimune." *"This action shall not remain unrevenged."*
*etymology*: "taqás" *from* "taqás" *(Arabic) = to revenge.*

## TAWAR

"tawar zadan" = *to talk rudely to, to treat rudely.*
"tup o tawar zadan" = *to reprimand someone.*
"Hamaw behew tup-o-tawar mizane." *"He constantly treats him rudely."* He hollers at him, and reprimands him."
"Tawar behew nazan!" *"Don't holler at her! Don't reprimand her!"*
*etymology:* √?

## TAXM

[*See* "axm". "Taxm" *always follows* "axm. *However it seems to be an independent word, not a rhyming meaningless word. cf* "taxm" *with* dam-aq, *(depressed, dejected).* dam, dame. तामस *támása (Sanskrit): dark.*]

## TÁQBÁZ

*This word means "in supine position". Thus* "Táqbáz xábid." *(He lay down in supine position.)*
[*etymology:* √? Táq, cf cártáq *(ajar/wide open)*(Dar o cártáq báz gozáwt o raft.)*(He left the door ajar/wide open and went out.) cf* "bar táq-a" *(The door is wide open.)(Vajguni dialect.)*]

## TÁTI

"táti kardan" = *to toddle,* "táti" = *toddling. This is a children's language word.*
[*etymology:* táti: *cf with English* "toddle, dodder, diddle. *"Indo-European base\* dheudh-, to shake, to whirl around confusedly.* ध् *dhu (Sanskrit) to shake, to agitate,* दूत *dhutá (shaken)*]

## TELOU TELOU

"Telou" *is usually used as* "telou telou xordan" *or* "telou telou zadan." *Both are intransitive verbs, meaning, to walk like drunkards.* "telou telou dádan" *(transitive verb = to swing something.)*
"Mast bud o telou telou mixord." *"He was drunk and had an unsteady gait."*

"Páw o ávizun karde, telou telou midád." *"He hung his legs down and swang them."*
[*etymology*: telou √?: *cf* celou: *thus*: ?? telou = tel-ou: tel, √?: ou = áb *(water)? to wave as water*]

## TER

*This is an onomatopoeic word. "Ter" is the diarrheal stool, evacuated with a loud noise and in a projectile fashion.*
"Be ter(r) oftáde." "Ter ter mizane": *(1- He has a bad dysentery or diarrhea. 2- He is in a predicament and he has lost control. He is in poor shape.)*
"Ter zadi!" *"You failed in a scandalous way!"*
"Salmuni be sar e bábá ter zad." *"The barber gave him a very bad haircut."*
"Be kár e má ter zad o raft." *"He ruined (messed up) our business and left."*

## TIPÁ, TIPPÁ

*This is a substantive, meaning "a kick with the forefoot."*
"Tipá zad tu káse kuzaw." *"He overturned his setup."*
"Tippá zad dar e kunew." *"He gave him a kick in the ass."*
[*etymology*: tipá = ti-pá: ti ≡ tok < nok, *cf* nok, nox, noxále, noxráz, noxri, *see* "noxále." *also cf* ti, tip *with English "tip", "top". Also see* "titi", *and* "tok" "pá" = *foot.*]

## TITI

*This is a word used to call birds and chickens to feed. Thus:*
"Faxr e Rázi elm rá liti konad　　　　　Piw e morqán rizad o titi konad."
"Fakhr e Razi *(the great Iranian scientist) makes a stew of sciences, and (he scatters it on the ground) and calls the chickens (his pupils) to come and feed on it."*
[*etymology*: titi = ti-ti: ti = tok, *cf* nouk < nox. < *mukhá* मुख *(Sanskrit) See* "tipá", *and* "noxále", *thus* ti, = tok = *the beak, bill*]

## TITIW

*In children's language, "titiw" is "clothes," "garment", usually new.* "Titiw mámániw geli wod." *"Her new dress was smeared with mud."*
etymology: tiw: *cf with English "tissue" and French "tissu": "tissue": middle English, a rich fabric. Old French pp of "tistre" "to weave < texere (Latin), √?*]

122

## TOBRE, TUBRE

"Tobre", *or* "tubre" *is a large cloth sack, carried on back or by hand.*
"Tobraw o endáxt ru kulew o raft." *"He flung his sack on his back and left."*
[*etymology:* √?]

## TOK

*This is a noun. It is a phonetic variant of* "nok" *(tip, top, beak, bill): See* "noxále", "titi".
"Raft tok e kuh." *"He went to the top of the mountain."*
"Juju tok mizane." *"The chicken pecks (at it)(with its beak)."*
"Tokew o cidan." *"1- They cut off its tip. 2- They snuffed it. 3- They rebuffed him, or rebuked him."*
[*etymology*: tok = nok, nouk: *see* "noxále," "tipá", "titi". nok < मुख *mukhá (Sanskrti).*]

## TONOK

*thin, sparse.*
*The correct pronunciation of this word is* "tanok". *It is an adjective. Anything spread over a large surface, thus diluted or low in density is* "tanok", *thus* "sparse, and thin."
"Sabziyá tonok wodan." *"The vegetable growth is thin or sparse."*
"Riwew tonok-e." *"His beard is thin, or sparse."*
[*etymology*: tonok = tanok = tan-uk; -uk, *a suffix.*
tan-, < tan-, (Avest): *to extend, make tense, expand.* tan-, *tanoti (Sanskrit):* (BQM p.524). तानः *tánáh: a thread, fiber;* तानं *tánán: expanse, extension;* तानवं *tánáván: thinness, smallness.*
*semantic reconstruction*: tonok, tanok: *cf:* ? tan-áb; tan-ew; tan-id-an; tang; tang e asb;]

## TOPOL

*plump, rotund.*
"Doxtar e topol mopol az áb darumad." *"The plump girl emerged from the water."*
[*etymology*: topol ≡ to-por =? tu + por *(full),* or: topol = top-ol = top = tup *(a ball)* -ol, = -ul, *(a suffix).* "topol" = *like a ball.*]

## TOPOQ

*This is a noun. It is almost always used as* "topoq zadan"*, meaning "to speak in a staccato fashion, with frequent pauses, or "ah's" and "eh's."*
"Cerá topoq mizani?" *"Why do you speak with frequent pauses?" "Why don't you speak fluently?"*
*etymology: ?*

## TOPOZ

"Topoz" *is a mace or a knobstick.*
"Ye topoz kardan tu kunew, dige xafe wod." *"(pejorative) They shoved a knobstick in his asshole, and he became quiet!"*
*etymology:* √?

## TORD

"Tord" *is an adjective. It is used to denote anything which is delicate and easily breakable. Customarily it is used primarily for foodstuff, such bread.*
"In nun e panjere xeyli tord-e." *"This cake is very fragile."*
"In xiyár tord-e." *"this cucumber is fresh and easily breakable, or fragile."*
[*etymology:* tord = tor-d, -d, *archaic suffix, cf* dus-t; *and* tor:? = tar *(fresh)*]

## TOXMI

"Toxmi" *is used in sense of anything shoddy, of low value or worthless.*
"Hame ye harfáw toxmi-ye." *"Whatever he says is idle-talk."*
"Ye máwin e toxmi xaride." *"He has bought a shoddy car."*
*etymology:* toxmi = toxm-i; toxm: *1- seed, 2- testis, 3-egg, 4- (fig.) anything to be despised is referred to* "toxm". *Thus if somebody has lost something or if he has suffered a loss, to console him one may say:* "Be toxmet!" *(literally)* "To your testis!" = "Hell with it!" "Don't care about it!" "Don't give a damn!"
[*etymology:* < √ taukman *(Old Iranian),* taokman *(Avest);* taumá *(Old Persian)(BQM p.476);* tuxm *(Pahlavi)(BF p.560)*]

## TOXS

*This is a substantive. It is used when referring to individuals who are stubborn and persevering in their efforts. One who repeatedly does something and does not give up.*
"Bacce ye toxsi-ye." *"He is a stubborn, persevering boy."*
"Toxs! az nardebun biyá páyin!" *"You stubborn boy, climb down the ladder!"*

124

[*etymology*: toxs: < tuxw, kuw: tuxwidan = kuwidan*: to struggle, to endeavor, to try hard, to work hard.*  Hutoxw; *a technician, a craftsman.*
t́vaxw *(Avest): zealous; tvákwás (Old Hindi)(power, strength) (BQM p.476).*
tuxwák *(Pahlavi)(energetic, hard-working)*(kuwá = toxs)*(BF p.560)*

## TRID

trid = tilit, telit = terit = tarit.
"Trid" *is a dish made as follows.  In a bowl of soup, buttermilk, or milk, dry bread crumb is mixed.  After all bread is soaked, it is eaten.  The dish thus fixed is called a* "trid".
"Trid e ábguwt bá ábduq-xiyár xordim."  *"We had a* "trid" *of porridge and buttermilk-cucumber drink."*
[*etymology*: trid, tarid, tar-id; tr-, = tar-, *cf* tar-ina: tar *(wet, moist).* tauruna *(Avest) (young).* táruna *(Old Hindi)(young);* tarr *(Pahlavi)(fresh). (BQM p.479)*

## TU

"Tu" *means "in, inside".*  "Biyá tu!"  *"Come in!";* "Bezár tuw!"  *"Put it inside."*
[*etymology*: "tu" *cf* dar, andar, अनतरे *antáre: (Sanskrit)(inside.)*]

## TUP O TAWAR

*See* "tawar".

## TUTULE

*See* "Atal matal tutule."

# U

## UR (1)

"Ur*" is used as* "ur ámadan", *or* "ur o ewve ámadan". *This means to exhibit a coquettish manner, to behave in a flirting manner. It is used primarily in reference to females.* "Doxtar e raqqqáse ye ur o ewveyi baráw miyumad ke un sarew nápeydá". *"The dancer girl made so much flirting movements in front of him."*

[*etymology*: "ur" *not related with Arabic* "ur" *(1- blind, 2- bare, naked). ur, (Persian)* √? *cf* urváh-man *(Pahlavi) (pleasant; enjoyable);* ur-váh-men-it-an *(Pahlavi)(to gladden)(BF p.563)*]

[urváh *most probably a Pahlavi loanword from hebzew: urvaxim.*]

## UR (2)

"Ur" *used only as* "loxt o ur", *means* "nude", naked".

"Doxtare loxt o ur parid ru miz." *"The girl stripped her clothes and leaped on the table."*

"Doxtará loxt o ur tu áb weno mikardan." *"The nude girls were swimming in the water."*

etymology: "ur" *from arabic* "ur" = nude.

# V

**VAQ**

1- "vaq zadan" = *to protrude (primarily for eyes)*
  "Cewáw vaq zade." *"His eyes are protruding."*
2- "vaq zadan" = *to bark*: "Sage vaq mizane." *"The dog barks."*
  *etymology:*
1- "vaq" *(protrusion): cf* vaqast *(clearly, evidently);* vaq-astan *(to make public)(BQM p.5041)*
2- "vaq" *(barking),* vak-, *sound;* váj; váź.

**VÁCORTIDAN**

"vácortidan" = *To wake up suddenly and be startled.*
"Bacce jiq zad, nane vácortid." *"The child screamed, and nanny woke up and was startled."*
*etymology:* vácortidan = vá-cort-id-an: vá-, *prefix* = *away, off,* -id-, = *verbal suffix or particle, signifying past tense,* -an, = *verbal suffix;* cort = *a nap. See* "cort"

**VÁSE**

"váse" = "bose" = *for, on the account of.*
"Bezár bosat (vásat) begam." *"Let me recount it for you."*
"Vásaw delvápasim." *"We are worried for him."*
*etymology:* váse = bose, vasnád = *for, on account of...*"vasnád e u" *"because of him, on his account"*
"Vasnád" *does not mean* "besyár", *in contrast to what is mentioned in the Persian dictionaries (BQM p.5027)*

**VÁVEYLÁ**

"Váveylá" *is used as an exclamatory remark. When something supposedly bad happens and one is expecting the ill consequences, one would say* "Váveylá!"
"Age pedaret befahme rufuze wodi, váveylá." *"If your father gets to know that you have flunked the exam, woe on you!"*

*etymology*: Vá! *(vocative particle)*, Váy!: "Váy bar to!", *"woe on you!"*; "veylá" vaila, veyle, vail *(Arabic): to wish evil for someone.* vayl *(Arabic): calamity, mishap, valley of hell. A word of threat or despair, Woe! Alas!*

## VEL

*Several meanings are given below:*
1- "vel kardan": *to give up, abandon, let go, let loose.*
   "Dastam o vel kon", *"Let go of my hand."*
   "Vel kon bábá asdollá." *"Come on! Don't give a damn!"*
   "Saga ro vel kard." *"He let the dog loose."*
2- "vel wodan": *to become loose, come off.*
   "Dastam vel wod." *"I lost (my) grip."*
3- "Velew!" *"Leave (him) alone!" "Give it up!" "Let him go!"*
   "velew" = be-hel-aw.
4- "vel": "Pesare tu xiyábuná vel-e." *"The lad is a vagabond."*
*etymology*: "Vel" *is most probably derived from* "váhel". "váhelidan = váhewtan" = vel< behel < helidan. "bil" = "bel" *(Lori dialect)* = behel = *let, allow. thus* "Bil bune!" *(Lori) = Let him see!*
hewtan = helidan: hiwtan *(Pahlavi):* √ harz-, *(Avest)*, herezenti *(to abandon)*, √ sarj-, srjáti *(Old Indian)*, herz *(Pahlavi – Ashkani). (BQM p.2339)*

## VELOU

"velou" = *scattered.*
"Gandomá hamaw velou wod." *"All the wheat was scattered about."*
"Ketábá ro tu ye otáq velou kard." *"He scattered the books on the floor."*
"Xeyli xaste budam, tu taxt velou wodam." *"I was exhausted, I collapsed on the bed."*
"Ye mowt xord velou wod." *"He received a punch and was knocked out."*
*etymology*: velou = vel-ou; vel, *see* "vel" –ou: √?

## VELVEWU

*See* "belbewu"

## VER(R)

"ver(r): *talking much, chattering.* "Hamaw ver mizane." *"He constantly chatters. He is a chatter-box."*
"Ver ver nakon (or: ver ver nazan)." *"Stop talking much!" "Stop chattering!"*

*Proverb:* "Pálunduzi-st o daryá ye elm, Áxundi nist o verr o verr." *"Making a felt-saddle needs lots of knowledge. It is not to be compared with Islamic clergy preaching nonsense."*
"Xeyli verráji kard." *"He talked much."*
"Verráji nakon." *"Don't talk much."*
*etymology*: verr: √?

## VEWGUN

*I believe this is the true form of the word used by the people, meaning "pinching". "vewgun gereftan" = "to pinch", ie to squeeze the flesh or skin between two fingers to cause pain. Also common is the form "niwgun". However "newkanj" is used rarely and only in the old literary works.*
"Tu bázár e Mehrán, mardá zaná o doxtará ro vewgun migiran." *Men pinch women or girls (while passing by them) in the Mehran marketplace."*
[*etymology: See "bew", "xow o bew".*
*In Persian dictionaries, "vewgun" and "niw-gun" are quoted as synonymous with "newkonj", or "newkanj". I believe this is not correct.*
"Newkanj" *is probably derived from:* ne-, ni-, *an old prefix,* = down, *and* "ewkanj", "wekanj" = crease, wrinkle. "Vewgun", *and* "niwgun" = "vew-gun", *and* "niw-gun", *respectively.* "vew" = "viw" = venom, ; "niw" = fang, *and* "-gun" *from* "gaona" *(Avest)* = (1- color; hue. 2- similar to; like). *Thus:* "niwgun", *and* "vewgun" *mean fang-like (bite-like) and venom-like respectively. also:* "viw" *(Pahlavi)* = 1- bite, 2- venom (BF p.612); "bew" = 1- aconitum, 2- pain, sorrow, 3- harm, 4- hostility (BF p.96 – MK p.18)]

## VIR

"Vir" *is used as either* "kasi rá vir gereftan", *or* "vir ámadan": *to do something as a whim.* "Virew gerefte musiqi bezane." *"He is now temporarily eager to play music."*
"Virew gerefte bere Faránse." *"He is now in a mood to go to France." (It is known that this is a temporary desire, it is nothing but a whim.)*
[*etymology*: vir. *cf* \*vira-, *(Avest);* vir, virák *(Pahlavi)(memory)(BQM p.2298).* "Ye kam virvir kon!" *(Fársuni-Lori dialect): try to remember.*]

## VUL, VULVUL

*see* "lul", *and* "lulidan". Vul, vulvul, vulvul zadan: *are synonyms of* "lul" "lul zadan" *and* "lulidan" *respectively.*

[*etymology*: vul = *lul*, लुल् *(Sanskrit)*: लोलती *loláti*, लुलित *lulitá*: *to roll about, to move to and fro, to toss about; -to shake, to stir, agitate*]

# W

## WAL

"Páw wal wode."  *"His leg is paralyzed."*

"Miwale." walidan *"He has a limp."* *"He limps."*

[*etymology*: "wal" = *limp, limping, paralyzed.* "walidan" = *to limp.* "Wal" *derived from Arabic* "wall" *to be dried up or disabled (hand), and* "vawall" *"to paralyze". (FM and BQM p.1287) (Student's Arabic English Dictionary 1974).*]

[*Cf* wal-vár; wal-ite; wal-anquze ; walang;walaxte;col; coláq; colman < "wal" *(Persian: lower limb)*](JGS)

## WALAM-WURBÁ = WALAM-WURVÁ

"Walam-wurbá: *refers to any "extremely confused or chaotic state."*

"Otáqew ce walam-wurbáyi-ye!" *"His room is in utter chaos."*

[*etymology*: walamwurbá = walam-wurbá; walam = walqam)*(BQM p.1289);* walam (Tabari) = *turnip.* wurbá = wurvá: vá = bá = *porridge < pac (Sanskrit),* pák (Pahlavi), pak (Avest): *to bake (BQM p.76)*

*I believe* "wur" *has nothing to do with "salty" (See BQM p.1307, in my belief, the impression is wrong).* wur ≡ xur ≡ har ≡ xor < xʹor: < √ xvar-, (Avest) = *to eat,* खट् khad (Sanskrit) = *to eat. or* wur ≡ wál ≡ wola ≡(wáli)*(rice), See* wolleqalamkár.

*As "turnip porridge" is made by mixing many different items, it is conceivable that it is used figuratively to refer to any "confused state of affairs."*]

## WALANG

walang = welang

*also see* "walang-taxte": "Bá walanghá ye boland ráh mire." *"He takes long strides."* "Walang mindáze ." *"He walks with long strides."*

[*etymology*: "wal-, = (thigh) (BQM p.1287,1289); cf.* wal-vár = *pants.;* walang-taxte; wal-ite *(a sort of puffy rural skirt);* wál-án-quze *(Gilani dialect)(a purse sewed in the waist-band of a pants.);* cal-pásak *(a lizard).*]

## WALANG-TAXTE

walang-taxte = welang-taxte

131

"walang-taxte" *used almost always with* "andáxtan": "Cerá welang-taxte mindázi?" (*Grammatically* "andáxtan *is superfluous*). *"Why do you walk with long strides and jumping movements?"*
[*etymology*: walang taxte = walang-táxte; "walang", *see* "walang": "taxte" = "táxte" *from* "táxtan": *to flow (vt), to make run, to attack.* "walang-táxte" = *to run or walk with long strides.*]

## WALAXTE
walaxte = welaxte
*This is a substantive. Its old meaning is not in common use now.* "Welaxte" = "walaxte" = *a kick with the tip of one's foot. To hit with a kick. Nowadays it is referred to any disorderly individual who would not place things in their right place. Any untidy individual who does not clean up the place or tings after use.*
"Doxtare ye welaxte raxtexábewam  jam-, nemikone!"  *"The untidy girl does not put her bed in order, either."*
[*etymology*: walaxte = wal-axt-e: *cf.* walang, wal-vár, wal-ite, wal-axu: *see* "walang": "wal = *leg, thigh*: axte = áxte = áhixte = *pulled, drawn. Thus:* "wal-axte", *1- a kick, 2- clumsy one, as though one who has no legs. cf* "axte" (*one who is castrated*)(*One, whose testis is extracted*).]

## WALAXU
*This is a noun. It refers to a special dance in southern provinces of Iran. This dance is remarkable by flinging and swinging one's legs around in long, jerky movements.*
"Ye doxtar umad walaxu raqsid." *"A young girl danced* walaxu-*style."*
[*etymology*: walaxu = wal-axu: "wal" *see:* "walang", "welaxte": -ax-u: √? < áxtan]

## WALÁL
*a loose stitch*
"In o walál bezan." *"Put loose stitches on this."*
etymology: ? < *Arabic:* "wallan" *to stitch clothes, to tack, to baste.*

## WAMAD
"Wamad" *is a sheet of homemade cotton fabric. It is commonly used as a bedsheet, or bedcover.*

"Wamad o sarew kewid o xábid." *"He covered himself with a "Shamad" and slept."*

[*etymology and semantic reconstruction:* wamad = wam-ad; -ad, *a suffix;* "wam" *cf* wám-e: *a membrane;* "vá-wám" = "bá-wám" *(a scarf, a head-dress)* "sám-ák-ce": *an apron.* √?: *"wám" = *"sám" = *a sheet, a membrane, a diaphragm.*]

## WAMBALEQURE

*This term is used as:*

1- *Referring to somebody wearing very grotesque and unseemly, incongruous pieces of garment, or*

2- *A handwriting, awfully bad with large crooked characters.*

"Cerá xodet o wambalequre kardi?" *"Why you are clothed so funny?"*

"Ye cizi wambalequre nevewt o dád dast e man." *"He wrote something in cat-scratch and handed it to me."*

[*eymology:* ? wambalequre – wambal-e-qur-e: *cf* wambal: *wámbárá* संबर *(Sanskrit) a demon;* qur-e = kur-e, *one who is blind*; wambale qure? = *a blind demon, a grotesque character.*]

## WANGUL

1- *Is the name of people in stories, for children and fables.*

"Ki xorde wangul e man? Ki xorde mangul e man?" *"Who has eaten up my children, named Shangul and Mangul?"*

2- *As a substantive,* "wangul" *means, happy, jolly, delightful.*

"Ye kami araq xorde wangul wode." *"He drank a little bit, and became delightful."*

"Doxtare wux o wanguli-ye." *"She is a witty and happy girl."*

[*etymology:* wang-ul: *cf* शंकर *wánkárá, and* शंकरी *wánkári: conferring happiness or prosperity, auspicious, propitious. Also used in India as the name of people eg:* Rávi Wankár.]

## WANQULAK-BÁZI

*Meaning "knavery", "knavishly". This word is used either alone or in combination with "darávardan". examples:* "Az in wangulakbázihá xowam nemiyáyad." *(I do not like (his) knavish manners.) or* "Cerá wanqulakbázi darmiyári?" *(Why do you behave knavishly?).*

[*etymology:* wanqul-ak, *see and cf* wangul]

133

## WAQ(Q)

waq(q) = wax
*See "six".*

## WÁF

*This is a noun. Formal meaning of "wáf" or "wiyáf" is a (rectal) suppository. Figuratively it is applied to individuals or things as a sign of depreciation, meaning "useless", or "something for which one has no use."*
"Mixáy begam dustam biyád?" "Biyád ce kárew konam?" "Wáfew konam?"
*"Do you want me to send my friend to you?" "What shall I do with him?" "He is good-for-nothing. I've no use for him."*
*etymology:* wáf = wiyáf: < *Arabic, a suppository.*

## WÁW

"wáw" = *urine:* "Wáw kard." = "Wáwid." = *"He pissed." "He urinated."*
"Wáw e xar" *"donkey's urine" alluding to "weak and lukewarm tea", or any insipid, weak, beverage, such as a bad beer.*
[*etymology:* √? *cf* शेष *wewán (Sanskrit): feces, residue.*]

## WAX

*See "waq(q)".*

## WILE-PILE

1- *Fibers, sinews and knots. This is used when referring to meat, for culinary purposes. Thus "In guwtam ke por e wile pila-s!" "This meat is (full of) sinews and knots (thus of poor quality)."*
2- *Figuratively it is used to refer to individuals who are not honest. A man who would profess something but act differently. One who is treacherous.*
[*etymology:* pile: *a tumor, an abscess, any round knot. cf* pel, pil, pewk, pewk-el, pesk, fes-qel. *"Pile" is also a cocoon, a ball, a bead, a knot.*
"wile" –wil-e: wil √? *cf* wil → riw-e
wile-pile: *roots and nodes.*]

## WIWAKI

*"Wiwaki" is a noun, which is almost always used with "bastan", as a verb.*
*"Wiwaki bastan", means that when somebody brags about his achievements, or specially when someone threatens somebody else, one produces a "wiwaki".*

*Thus one would put one hand on one's mouth sideways and exhales from between pressed lips, producing a high tone noise, similar to a fart. The act of "Wiwaki bastan" means that "your threats causes no fear", or "your claim is worthless."*

"Wáh goft bedin jallád bekowatew." "Dalqak bará ye wáh wiwaki bast." *"The king said, let the executioner behead him." "The clown made a* wiwaki, *for the Shah."*

[*etymology:* wiwaki √?:

wiw-kabáb: wiw-lik; wiw-ak; "wiwak" *also cf with "sausage". Also probably* wiw in wiwaki;

"wiw-ak": शिशु *wiwu (Sanskrit): 1- a child, an infant, 2- the young of any animal, 3- a boy under 8 years of age.*]

## WOL

"Tanáb wol wod." *"The rope became slack."*

"Cerá wol umadi?" *"Why did you give up?"*

"Dastam wol wod." *"My grip became loose and I gave up."*

"Xamir wol wod." *"The dough became loose."*

[*etymology: See* "col".

चल्ल् *cil, cel: to become or be loose or slack, to act wantonly.*

चलित *calita: loose.*]

## WOLLE-QALAMKÁR

*Usually used as* "áw e wolle-qalamkár". *This is a noun. Literally it means "a porridge made of rice and cabbage". Figuratively it is used in reference to anything made of too many nonhomogeneous components. Thus one may propose a plan for improving the financial situation of a company. If the plan is made of several incongruous parts without reasonable background and interrelationship, one may say* "In ke yek áw e wolleqalamkár-e!" *(This is a hodgepodge!)*

[*etymology and semantic reconstruction:*

wolle: < शालिः *wálih (Sanskrit) (rice); also compare with* "wáli" "wálizár";

"wollezard"; celou; wur-bá *(a porridge made with rice);* wurbá; wolleqalamkár

qalam = kalam *(cabbage)*

-kár: *cf* kári: *compare with "chicken curry" (English);* "kufte-kári" *(a meatball curry)*]

# X

## XADANG

*This is an adjective.  Anything erect, stiff, tough and straight is* "xadang".
"Yek tir e xadang."  *"A straight and stiff arrow"*
*etymology:* √?

## XALÁ

*This is a noun, meaning "a restroom" a "W.C."*
"Goft saret o bezan be sang e xalá."  *"He said "hit your head against the sink of the rest-room."  (a pejorative way, to get rid of the headache.)*
*etymology:* √?

## XAR-COSONE

A dung beetle, a blasp.  *see* "cosone"
"Xar-cosone" *is a depreciative term, referred to a despicable person.*
"Donyá ro bebin ce pis-e --- xarcosone rayis-e!" *literally: "See how bad is the condition of the world. A dung beetle is the chief." meaning: You despicable person!*

## XARXAWE

*See* "qewqere"

## XER

"Xer" *is a noun meaning the front part of the neck.  By extension "the trachea".  Also* "xer-xere" *means: throat, trachea.*
"Xerew o begir o bebar!"  *"Get hold of him by the neck and take him there (by force)!"*
"Xerew o borid."  *"He cut its throat."*
"Tá xerxere zir e qarz-e."  *"He is deep/throat-deep in debt."*
[*etymology:* xer: *cf* कृक् krikáh: *the throat.*]

## XER-XERE

*See* "xer".

## XEWTAK

*This is a noun, meaning a gusset in the form of a diamond sewn at the crotch of a pants.*
"Xewtakew páre wode." *(literally)* *"The crotch-gusset of his pants is torn."*
"Xewtakew páre wode." *figuratively:* *"He had a very hard time, dealing with a very tough problem."*
"Xewtakew o páre kard." *(literally)* *"He tore off (ripped off) the gusset of his pants." (figuratively) "He gave him a very tough time."*
[*etymology*: xewtak = xewt-ak: xewt: *a block; a mud-brick*; xiwt *(Pahlavi)*; iwtya-, *(Avest) (BQM p.750)*; इष्टिका *iwtiká*, इष्ठक: *iwtaká (Sanskrit) a brick.*]

## XIT

"Xit" *is almost comparable to* "bur". "Xit" *is used wither with* "wodan" *or* "kardan". "Xit kardan": *to prove someone wrong and to disgrace him.*
"Xub xitew kardam." *"I proved him wrong and disgraced him."*
"Xit wodan": *to be proven wrong and to be disgraced or embarrassed.*
"Raftam az áb bekewamew birun, ammá didam xub wená mikone, xit wodam."
*"I was going to rescue him, but he started swimming well, I was proven wrong in my assumption and I was embarrassed."*
*etymology*: √?

## XOL

*Also see* "xole", "cel", "xol o cel". "Xol" *is a substantive.* "Pesarew xol-e."
*"His son is an idiot."* "Doxtare xol o cel-e". *"Her daughter is of low intelligence and of loose character."* "Cerá xolbázi darmiyári?" *"Why do you behave irrationally?"*
[*etymology*: xol: *cf* xahl, xváhl: *not straight, crooked, bent. Also* "koule" *fits closely in the basic concept of "crooked, bent, not straight." √?*]

## XOLE

"xole" *crooked, bent, not straight. See* "xol", "pate xole".

## XORNÁS

*This is a noun.* "Xornás" *means snoring, roaring and growling.*
"Pire mard xábide xornás mikewe." *"The old man is sleeping and snoring."*
"Sage xornás kewid." *"The dog growled."* "Xornás kewidan" = *to snore, to roar, to growl.*

*Also note* "pofnás": *"puffing" while sleeping.*
[*etymology*: xornás = xor-nás: xor:? *onomatopoeic origin. cf* xraos *(Avest)(to cry),* xrus *(a rooster);* nás = *nose* √ नासा *násá (Sanskrit)(a nose). Also cf* náz; nos, nowxár.]

## XOW O BEW

*See* "bew".

## XUR

"Xur" *only used in the following proverb.* "Xar o bá xur mixore, morda ro bá gur." *It is applied to people who overeat and use no discretion in their choice of food. Literally:* "He eats the donkey with the sack and the dead man with his tomb/coffin/."
[*etymology*: "xur" = *a burlap? sack (Dehkhoda's Proverbs and Aphorisms). The sack of hay hanging on a donkey's neck. cf* áxor = *stable,* á-xv́ar *(Pahlavi):* á-kv́ará *(Avest)(BQM p.19) (BF p.75).*]

# Y

## YÁLQUZ

"Yálquz" *is a substantive.  It means an individual who is not married.  One who has no family or dependents, thus enjoying freedom of movement and action.*  "Yálquze, har já bere jáw-e."  *"He is single, and unmarried, wherever he goes, he is at home."*
*etymology:* < "yálquz" *(Turkish)(alone).*

## YÁRU

"Yáru" *functions as a pronoun, denoting a certain third person singular. Thus:* "Yáru raft."  *"A certain man or woman went away."  "A so-and-so left."* "Yáru dak wod."  *"A so-and-so left surreptitiously."*
[*etymology:* "yáru = yár-u; -u *(suffix);* yár *(a friend, comrade.)* ayár *(Pahlavi).]*

## YEK HOU

"Yek hou", *or* "ye hou" *means "all of a sudden".*  "Ye hou zad zir e xande." *"All of a sudden he burst into a laughter."*  "Ye hou umad tu ."  *"Suddenly he came in."*
*etymology:* "hou" √?

## YEKKE

"Yekke xordan"  *"to be shocked".*  "Az didan e man tu otáqew yekke xord." *"He was shocked, when he found me in his room."*  "Az xabar e zanáwuyi ye mádarew yekke xord."  *"He was shocked by the news of his mother's marriage."*
*etymology:* √?

## YEKKE BEDOU

"Yekke be dou kardan": *to argue*
"Bá man yekke be dou mikone."  *"He argues with me."*
*etymology:* yekke, one, alone.; dou? < doyidan *(Pahlavi): to speak loudly, holler, to argue, used for demonic creatures. (BF 174)*

## YELXI

*This is an adverb. Meaning: Not according to standard methods or rules. Not following a correct way or manner.*

*examples*: "Yelxi bár umade." *(He has grown up without proper education.)* "Yelxi sáz mizane." *(He plays music not according to correct method. He has learned it without proper education.)* "Yelxi kár mikone." *(He works improperly, not according to standard rules and methods.)*

[*etymology*: yelxi, *cf* harz, harze, qalat, alaki, xol, xal, xahl, xvile, xaráb, < harediw *(Avest)* (harak); arak *(Pahlavi); also* "xarak" *as in* "xormá-xarak"]

## YENGE

*The formal meaning of* "yenge" *is bride's maid. In Tehrani dialect, and slang use,* "yenge" *means someone who accompanies a person and causes trouble. a nuisance. a chaperon.*

"Yenge nemixám!" *"I don't need a company who is going to be a burden on me."*

"Yenge kewidan": *To carry someone or something uselessly with oneself. An action considered unnecessary and cumbersome under certain circumstances.* "Xodew o be xune ye kadxodá ráh nemidahand, yenge ham mikewe." *"He is not welcome to the home of the village headman, despite this he is taking additional people accompanying him to there!"*

*etymology*: yenge: *(Turkish): best man, bride's maid. (FM p.5271)*

## YENGE DONYÁ

"Yenge donyá" *means a place, or a country very far away and across the oceans. Nowadays it is typically used to denote the U.S.A. Although any part of the American Continent would qualify as* "yenge donyá".

"Táze az yenge donyá umade." *"He has just come from the U.S.A."*

*etymology*: yenge donyá: *Turkish.*

## YOQOR

"Yoqor" *is an adjective. Anything coarse, and unshapely is* "yoqor."

"Páyehá ye in miz xeyli yoqor-e." *"The legs of this table are very thick and coarse."*

"Dastáw yoqor-e." *"His hands are very thick and unshapely."*

*etymology*: ? < yoqun *(Turkish)(thick).*

# Z

## ZANGI

*This is a substantive. It is depreciative. It means a negro (noun or adjective). A related term is "barzangi" (pejorative)(a short form for "abar-zangi" = A very black negro. (figuratively) an ugly dark-skinned individual, (The nigger is very proud.)*
*"Barzangi xeyli fisu-e." "The ugly dark-skinned (man, or woman) is very proud."*
*"Yá zangi ye zang o yá rumi ye rum." "Either full negro or pure white (Roman) blood." (figuratively) Either of the two extremes, nothing in between.*
*etymology: zangi. cf zang, zangbár. zang-ik (Pahlavi): a negro. √?*

## ZAQNABUT

*This is a vocative term. When somebody makes a statement which is not to the liking of the other individual, he or she may exclaim: "Zaqnabut!". Meaning that I don't like your statement, remark or prophesy. It is a jocular term, used for people one knows and who are on close friendly terms. It is neither pejorative, nor depreciative.*
*"Eláhi bárun biyád, natuni beri birun." "Zaqnabut!" "May it rain hard so you can't go out!" "Zaqnabut!" (Hell with your statement.)*
*Also when somebody chuckles, somebody else may say "Zaqnabut!" to stop his/her chuckling.*
*etymology: zaqnabut = zaq-nabut: zaq cf zaqqum (Arabic) 1- A tree growing in the hell, bearing a very bitter fruit. 2- Anything bitter and poisonous.*
*also cf zaq: zarx (Gilaki): bitter, taxl (Pahlavi)(bitter); nabut √?*
*also: zaq cf záq, zák = alum; nabut? cf nabát: crystal (candy).*

## ZARDANBU

*"Zardanbu", or "zardambu", is a substantive. It means sallow and yellowish. A sickly yellow hue of the skin. "Hame riqu o zardambu budan." "They were all puny, and sallow." "Taryáki ye zardambu…" "The yellow-hued opium-addicted man…"*
*etymology: zardambu = zard-ambu: zard (yellow); ambu √?*

## ZÁQ-SIYÁ

*This term is only used as "záq siyá ye kasi ro cub zadan." This means to follow somebody and spy on him. To pry into somebody's affairs.*

"Cerá záq siyá ye doxtara ro cub mizani?" *"Why you follow this girl and spy on her?"*

*etymology:* √?: siyá = siyáh =black; záq: 1- zág *(Alum, vitriol),* 2- *a crow.* zaq *(Pahlavi) (crow)(BF p.654).* záq-siyá = *a black crow. (figuratively:* záq-siyá = *(black crow) = somebody's shadow, thus to follow somebody.)*

## ZEBEL

*"Zebel" is a substantive. It is used to describe a person who is very smart, and who uses the circumstances to his benefit.*

"Bacce ye zebeli-ye." *"He is a shrewd child."*

"Be qaddew nigá nakon, xeyli zebel-e." *"Don't look at his size. He is very shrewd."*

[*etymology:* zebel, *cf* cábok: *cf.* चापलं *cápálán,* चापल्य *cápályá (Sanskrit) quick motion, swiftness, rashness, cf* "sabok", *cf* sap-uk *(Pahlavi) 1- light, 2- nimble.*]

## ZEH ZADAN

*"Zeh zadan" means to fail badly either due to fear or due to one's incapability to cope with a big task.*

"Yáru zeh zad, natunest diplomew o begire." *"He failed very badly, he could not graduate from the school."*

*etymology:* "zeh" *has several meanings. The one most compatible with slang* "zah zadan", *is "to exude" "exudation". Figuratively when somebody is awfully scared, one may lose control of urine and feces. This may be taken figuratively as a sign of extreme fear, anxiety and failure in a big task.*

## ZEKI

"Zeki!", *and* "Zekise!" *are exclamatory remarks. When somebody states something or threatens to take an action, one would say:* "Zeki!", *or* "Zekise!" *meaning that your statement is worth nothing.*

"Mizanam dak o dandat o xurd mikonamá!" "Zeki!", *or* "Zekise!" *"I'll crush your neck!" "Hell with you!"*

*etymology: Quoting Professor Manuchehr Varasteh,* "zeki", *and* "zekise" *are words derived from Arabic* "ďakiyyon ́va kayyeson!" (ذکیَّ و کیسَّ). *These Arabic words, are used as an exclamation, meaning "Very intelligent!"*

*Persians have used these terms, in a depreciative, and pejorative sense. Also compare with* "mofti". dakiy ذكى *(Arabic): to be sagacious.*

## ZEKISE

*See* "zeki".

## ZEL

zel = zil

"Zel", *or* "zil" *is used only when referring to meat. Any red, hard, fatless meat which is not easily cooked is called* "zel".

"In guwt ke zelle zell-e." *"This is a bad meat. It is red, fatless and hard." As a matter of fact* "zel" *is a tailless sheep, the meat of which is inferior to those with fatty tails.*

*etymology:* √?

## ZELLE

"zelle wodan" *"to be harassed."* "zelle kardan" *"to harass".*

"Man o zelle kard." *"He harassed me." "He wore me off by constantly annoying me."*

"Dige zelle wodam, pul o behew dádam." *"I was harassed, so I gave him the money."*

*etymology:* "zelle" *probably from Arabic:* "zell": *to be low, weak, obscure, base, or* "zalil" *(Arabic): humble, vile, despised, contemptible.*

## ZEQ, ZEQ-ZEQ

"zeq", "zeq-zeq", "zeq-(zeq) zadan" = *nagging, to nag, respectively.*

"Zeq (zeq) nazan!" *"Stop nagging."*

*etymology:* zeq: *cf* żak, żak-id-an: *to mumble, and grumble. To complain by grumbling. also cf* "zer" *also cf* "zaqár" *(crying, shouting)* = żaqár < ? *jqár *(Soghdian), xżqer (Soghdian)(to call)(FM p.1776, BQM p.1059)*

## ZER, ZER-ZER

"Zer" *or* "zer-zer" *means* "whining, crying".

"Zer-zer e bacce xafam kard." *"The baby's crying, got on my nerves."*

"Zer-(zer) zadan", *or* "kardan": *to cry, to whine.*

"Bacce zer-(zer) mizane." *"The child cries".*

"Bacce ye zer-zeru!" *"Cry-baby!"*

*etymology*: "Zer" *is most probably an onomatopoeic word. also cf* "zeq".

## ZERT

"Zert" *is a noun.*
"Zertew qamsur wod." *(He/she/it was ruined/devastated. He failed very badly. He was defeated. It failed catastrophically.)* "Zertew darumad." *(It broke down. It failed very badly. It broke down and smashed into pieces.)*
[*etymology*: qamsur: *see* "qamsur" *(equivalent of* "kamzur")*(without strength; weak; powerless);*
zert: *cf* zereda *(Avest)(heart)*
*thus* "Zertew qamsur wod." *(literally: His heart was rendered powerless.)*
"Zertew darumad." *(It broke down and its heart (its inside) came out.)*]

## ZIL

*See* "zel".

## ZIPOU, ZIPPOU

"In cáyi ke zippou-s." *"This tea is very weak."*
"Áb e zippou ávorde mige cáyi-ye." *"He brought me a cup of water, and claimed that it were tea."*
[*etymology*: zipou = zip-ou: zip = sup: *any clear liquid food.* सूपः *supáh (Sanskrit) broth, soup.* "ou" = "áb" *(water)*: zip-ou, *literally "soup water" clear, watery soup.*]

## ZOHM

"zohm" = "zoxm"
"Zohm" *is a stench of either rotten butter, or a smell of fresh fish, or occasionally meat.* "Kare buy e zohm gerefte (*or*, mide)." *"The butter stinks. It is gone bad."* *The smell of dishes soiled with soft-boiled egg is also called* "zohm."
"Buy e zohm e máhi." *"The smell of (fresh) fish."*
"Estekán bu ye zohm mide." *"The glass smells of egg."*
*etymology*: zohm *(Arabic)(FM p.1766),* "zehmat" = "zohm" *(BQM p.1049)*

## ZOL, ZOL-ZOL

"Zol" *is always used as* "zol(-zol) zadan" *meaning "to stare at", "to ogle.", "to glare".*

144

"Ye káre váysáde be man zol zade."  *"He is staring at me, as though he's got nothing else to do."*
"Pesare zol zade be doxtare."  *"The young man is staring at the girl."  "the lad is ogling the girl."*
*etymology:* √?

## ZOQ (1), ZOQ-ZOQ

"Angowtam zoq-zoq mikone (*or,* mizane)."  *"My finger throbs."  "I have a throbbing pain in my finger."*
"Dandunew zoq-zoq mikone."  *"He has a throbbing toothache."*
"zoq (-zoq) zadan" (*or* kardan) = *to throb, to have a throbbing pain.*
[*etymology:* "zoq" *is of the same root as* "six", "sok", *and* "waq", *and* "soqolme." *See* "six, sok, waq, soqolme".]

## ZOQ (2)

"Tu ye zoq(q) e kasi zadan" *(Give somebody the brush-off.)*
[*etymology:* "Zoq" *is commonly thought to be derived from Arabic* "zouq" (ذوق) *(taste, relish). Note that in colloquial Persian one never says* "Tu ye zouq e kasi zadan". *Instead one always says* "Zadam to zoqqew!" *(I gave him a brush-off!)*
Zoq *cf.* "socati", "sucyati" *(Sanskrit)(to shine, glow, burn, hurt badly, sadden), cf* "saocint-" *(burning),* átre-saoka-, *(firebrand),* saoka. *Thus* "Tu ye zoqq e kasi zadan" *"Kill somebody's fire /light/ thus feelings."*]

## ZOXM

*See* "zohm".

Other books written by the author on Language
کتابهای دیگر از این نویسنده در زمینه ی زبان
\*\*\*\*\*\*\*\*\*\*\*\*\*\*\*\*\*\*\*\*\*\*\*\*\*\*\*\*\*\*\*\*\*\*\*\*\*\*\*\*
از "عجم" تا "پارسی"
کالبد شناسی سنجشی زبان عجم (فارسی نوین) و پارسی

## From "Lingua Ambigua" to the "Persian Language"
A comparative anatomy of the "Lingua Ambigua" and the Persian Language
written in Persian
\*\*\*\*\*\*\*\*\*\*\*\*\*\*\*\*\*\*\*\*\*\*\*\*

کارنامه ی پارسیک
راهنمای واژه سازی بشیوه ی دانشیک

## Karname Ye Parsik
A Scientific Study of the Persian Verbal Stems and Derivatives
written in Persian
\*\*\*\*\*\*\*\*\*\*\*\*\*\*\*\*\*\*\*\*\*\*\*\*

## Persian Language in Phonetic Alphabet
An Introductory Course for Foreigners
\*\*\*\*\*\*\*\*\*\*\*\*\*\*\*\*\*\*\*\*\*\*\*\*

واژه نامه ی زبان کوچه ی پارسی

## A Glossary of Slang Persian Words
Persian words in phonetic alphabet
With Etymologic and Semantic Remarks
\*\*\*\*\*\*\*\*\*\*\*\*\*\*\*\*\*\*\*\*\*\*\*\*

## A Concise Etymologic Dictionary of the Persian Language
شناسنامه ی واژگان پارسی
Volume I (A to I)
Volume II (J to T)
Volume III (U to Z) & Index
Persian words in phonetic alphabet
\*\*\*\*\*\*\*\*\*\*\*\*\*\*\*\*\*\*\*\*\*\*\*\*

فرهنگ پند و دستان پارسی
(پند و دستان یاب)
بر پایه برداشت پیامها

## Dictionary of Persian Proverbs and Aphorisms
\*\*\*\*\*\*\*\*\*\*\*\*\*\*\*\*

A Comparative Probe in the Iranian Dialects and Semilanguages
Dialects and Semilanguages in phonetic alphabet

*****************

زربیز پارسی

Zarbiz e Pársi

An English-Persian Lexicon
Volume I: Word Finder
Volume II: Sections P (prefixes), M (mesofixes), S (suffixes), C (concept)
Volume III: Section L (lexicon)
Persian written in phonetic alphabet
******************************

www.ingramcontent.com/pod-product-compliance
Lightning Source LLC
Chambersburg PA
CBHW050352100426
42739CB00015BB/3373